"Historically, religious life has been boratory of change in the church. S U.S. religious congregations have ... the way in implementing the vision of Vatican II and in adapting the church's ministry to contemporary realities. The challenge today, however, is even greater: to live out of a transforming love of God and commitment to God's people, and, in that light, to invent a future for religious life in the 21st century that breaks with our pattern of linear change. This task will require rethinking every aspect of religious life, as well as the relationship of the religious life to other callings in the church. Sister Catherine has given us a good starting point for the work that lies ahead."

Doris Gottemoeller, R.S.M.
President, Sisters of Mercy of the Americas

"A paradigm is not a blueprint, and in this clear and sharp distillation of the searching of religious in the past several decades, Catherine Harmer has the wisdom to sort out prophecy and prediction. Today's call, she believes, is to 'reinvent the future' with trust in God, but also with sensitivity to the paradigm shift that requires nothing less than a radical transformation of outlook and strategies.

"The chapters that treat of global consciousness and mission, and with organization and structure, are among the finest I have seen. Drawing on her own rich experience of leadership, the author deals effectively with most of the themes and issues that preoccupy women and men religious. Members looking for sane guidance toward the future, as well as lay leaders and clergy who are increasingly collaborating with them, will find here an austerely hopeful way of advancing into the next century."

Thomas E. Clarke, S.J.
Author, Theologian
Associate Editor, *The Way*

"The future of 'religious life' (and within a very short time it may not be called that) is placed squarely in the midst of the revolutionary transformations that characterize the human agenda today. Catherine Harmer invites us to explore the challenge of moving from linear thinking and action (the 'maintenance modes' so common today among religious) to creativity and deep trust in God: 'If religious life still has something to offer the people of God, then it will be transformed and will continue.' We religious are the agents of this transformation! Living in the midst of one of the major paradigm shifts of human history is not always comfortable, but it *is* exciting. The land of Canaan beckons...."

Paula Gonzalez, S.C.
Futurist, Director of *Earth Connection*

RELIGIOUS LIFE

in the

21st Century

A Contemporary
Journey
into Canaan

Catherine M. Harmer

TWENTY-THIRD PUBLICATIONS

Mystic, CT 06355

The Scripture used in this volume is from the New Revised Standard Version Bible, copyright 1989, Division of Christian Education of the National Council of the Churches of Christ in the United States of America. All rights reserved.

Twenty-Third Publications
185 Willow Street
P.O. Box 180
Mystic, CT 06355
(203) 536-2611
800-321-0411

ISBN 0-89622-651-4
Library of Congress Catalog Card Number 95-60063

Printed in the U.S.A.

To the many religious,
women and men,
who have made the journey through the desert,
that they may have the courage
to take the next steps into the future,
into Canaan.

ACKNOWLEDGMENTS

I want to thank all those who have been part of my journey and who contributed in a variety of ways to the birthing of this book.

Over the years I have been privileged to work with many religious women and men as consultant, facilitator, and trainer. Such relationships are always two-way, both sides giving and receiving, teaching and learning, challenging and inspiring. The ideas that eventually became a book were seeded, frequently watered, and often challenged by those religious. It is in the exchange, back and forth, that concepts are tested, questioned, affirmed, built on, and sometimes sadly put aside.

My own community, Medical Mission Sisters, has been a great source of encouragement throughout the years, as well as of challenge. The experiences of living and working in several countries, the incredible educational opportunities, and the many conversations over the years have crafted both the person I am and the things I have been able to do. Not least, I want to thank the community for being willing to give me the time to write and for cheering me on, accepting the costs. To my own local "cluster" of sisters and associates I want to give special thanks for understanding why it was so important for me at this time to write and *not* do some other things.

It is important also to thank my family, who without really understanding what I was doing, have been a base of support over the years. I especially need to thank my parents, both now deceased, who through their words and example instilled in me at a very early age a love of reading that has opened incredible worlds to me.

And to you, the reader, thank you for trying me out. I hope you will find it worth your time.

A special thanks is due to the people of Twenty-Third Publications, who so quickly responded positively to my efforts and were so warm and affirming of what I had written. They made the process from initially detaching myself enough to mail the manuscript, through the additions and revisions, an actual pleasure!

CONTENTS

RELIGIOUS
LIFE
in the
21st Century

Journey to Canaan

"See what kind of land it is."

The Lord said to Moses, "Send men to spy out the land of Canaan, which I am giving to the Israelites; from each of their ancestral tribes you shall send a man, every one a leader among them." So Moses sent them from the wilderness of Paran, according to the command of the Lord, all of them leading men among the Israelites. Moses sent them to spy out the land of Canaan, and said to them, "Go up there into the Negeb, and go up into the hill country, and see what the land is like, and whether the people who live in it are strong or weak, whether they are few or many, and whether the land they live in is good or bad, and whether the towns that they live in are unwalled or fortified, and whether the land is rich or poor, and whether there are trees in it or not. Be bold, and bring some of the fruit of the land." Now it was the season of the first ripe grapes.

So they went up and spied out the land from the wilderness of Zin to Rehob, near Lebo-hamath. They went up into the Negeb, and came to Hebron; and Ahiman, Sheshai, and Talmai, the Anakites, were there. (Hebron was built seven years before Zoan in Egypt.) And they came to the Wadi Eshcol, and cut down from there a branch with a single cluster of grapes, and they carried it on a pole between two of them. They also brought some pomegranates and figs. That place was called the Wadi Eshcol, because of the cluster that the Israelites cut down from there.

At the end of forty days they returned from spying out the land. And they came to Moses and Aaron and to all the congregation of the Israelites in the wilderness of Paran, at Kadesh; they brought back word to them and to all the congregation, and showed them the fruit of the land. And they told him, "We came to the land to which you sent us; it flows with milk and honey, and this is its fruit. Yet the people who live in the land are strong, and the towns are fortified and very large; and besides, we saw the descendants of Anak there. The Amalekites live in the land of the Negeb; the Hittites, the Jebusites, and the Amorites live in the hill country; and the Canaanites live by the sea, and along the Jordan."

But Caleb quieted the people before Moses, and said, "Let us go up at once and occupy it, for we are well able to overcome it." Then the men who had gone up with him said, "We are not able to go up against this people, for they are stronger than we." So they brought to the Israelites an unfavorable report of the land that they had spied out, saying, "The land that we have gone through as spies is a land that devours its inhabitants; and all the people that we saw in it are of great size. There we saw the Nephilim (the Anakites come from the Nephilim); and to ourselves we seemed like grasshoppers, and so we seemed to them."

Then all the congregation raised a loud cry, and the people wept that night. And all the Israelites complained against Moses and Aaron; the whole congregation said to them, "Would that we had died in the land of Egypt! Or would that we had died in this wilderness! Why is the Lord bringing us into this land to fall by the sword? Our wives and our little ones will become booty; would it not be better for us to go back to Egypt?" So they said to one another, "Let us choose a captain, and go back to Egypt."

Then Moses and Aaron fell on their faces before all the assembly of the congregation of the Israelites. And Joshua son of Nun and Caleb son of Jephunneh, who were among those who had spied out the land, tore their clothes and said to all the congregation of the Israelites, "The land that we went through as spies is an exceedingly good land. If the Lord is pleased with us, he will bring us into this land and give it to us, a land that flows with milk and honey. Only, do not rebel against the Lord; and do not fear the people of the land, for they are no more than bread for us; their protection is removed from them, and the Lord is with us; do not fear them." But the whole congregation threatened to stone them.

Then the glory of the Lord appeared at the tent of meeting to all the Israelites. And the Lord said to Moses, "How long will this people despise me? And how long will they refuse to believe in me, in spite of all the signs that I have done among them? I will strike them with pestilence and disinherit them, and I will make of you a nation greater and mightier than they."

But Moses said to the Lord, "Then the Egyptians will hear of it, for in your might you brought up this people from among them, and they will tell the inhabitants of this land. They have heard that you, O Lord, are in the midst of this people; for you, O Lord, are seen face to face, and your cloud stands over them and you go in front of them, in a pillar of cloud by day and in a pillar of fire by night. Now if you kill this people all at one time, then the nations who have heard about you will say, 'It is because the Lord was not able to bring this people into the land he swore to give them that he has slaughtered them in the wilderness.' And now, therefore, let the power of the Lord be great in the way that you promised when you spoke, saying,

'The Lord is slow to anger,
and abounding in steadfast love,

> forgiving iniquity and transgression,
> but by no means clearing the guilty,
> visiting the iniquity of the parents
> upon the children
> to the third and the fourth generation.'

Forgive the iniquity of this people according to the greatness of your steadfast love, just as you have pardoned this people, from Egypt even until now."

Then the Lord said, "I do forgive, just as you have asked; nevertheless—as I live, and as all the earth shall be filled with the glory of the Lord—none of the people who have seen my glory and the signs that I did in Egypt and in the wilderness, and yet have tested me these ten times and have not obeyed my voice, shall see the land that I swore to give to their ancestors; none of those who despised me shall see it. But my servant Caleb, because he has a different spirit and has followed me wholeheartedly, I will bring into the land into which he went, and his descendants shall possess it. Now, since the Amalekites and the Canaanites live in the valleys, turn tomorrow and set out for the wilderness by the way to the Red Sea."

And the Lord spoke to Moses and to Aaron, saying: "How long shall this wicked congregation complain against me? I have heard the complaints of the Israelites, which they complain against me. Say to them, 'As I live,' says the Lord, 'I will do to you the very things I heard you say: your dead bodies shall fall in this very wilderness; and of all your number, included in the census, from twenty years old and upward, who have complained against me, not one of you shall come into the land in which I swore to settle you, except Caleb son of Jephunneh and Joshua son of Nun. But your little ones, who you said would become booty, I will bring in, and they shall know the land that you have despised. But as for you, your dead bodies shall

fall in this wilderness. And your children shall be shep-
herds in the wilderness for forty years, and shall suffer for
your faithlessness, until the last of your dead bodies lies in
the wilderness. According to the number of the days in
which you spied out the land, forty days, for every day a
year, you shall bear your iniquity, forty years, and you
shall know my displeasure'" (Numbers 13:1–3,17–33;14:1–
34).

When he came to Nazareth, where he had been brought
up, he went to the synagogue on the sabbath day, as was
his custom. He stood up to read, and the scroll of the
prophet Isaiah was given to him. He unrolled the scroll
and found the place where it was written:

"The Spirit of the Lord is upon me,
    because he has anointed me
    to bring good news to the poor.
He has sent me to proclaim release
    to the captives
    recovery of sight to the blind,
    to let the oppressed go free,
    to proclaim the year of the Lord's favor."

And he rolled up the scroll, gave it back to the attendant,
and sat down. They eyes of all in the synagogue were fixed
on him. Then he began to say to them, "Today this scripture has been fulfilled in your hearing." All spoke well of
him and were amazed at the gracious words that came
from his mouth. They said, "Is not this Joseph's son?"(Luke
4:16–22)

Introduction

"They shall appreciate the land you have spurned."

As a child in a Catholic school the story of the Israelites wandering in the desert for forty years made no sense to me. After all, a glimpse of the maps in our Bible study books would show how short a distance it was from Egypt to Canaan. And they were nomads, so they must have known their way around the desert. Even walking, with the animals and the children, it should not have taken them forty years. Later I came to know that it had to do with being unfaithful to God. However, even as an adult, I tended to recall the unfaithfulness as the worship of the golden calf.

Recently, while reading the passage from Numbers at an early morning Mass I suddenly saw the whole thing in a different way; it was a combination of the fear coming out of one's perceptions of reality and a lack of trust in God. I still remember that morning when it all fell together, when I gained an insight into religious life today and for the future.

Often we look at religious life from a variety of perspectives: sociological, psychological, organizational, canonical, political, spiritual. Any and all of the perspectives have something to say to us. When we look into the possible future of religious life, into the 21st century and beyond, all of these disciplines have something to offer. In numerous works over the past decade there have been analyses of what has been, what is now occurring in religious life, what the future might or might not be. Reading these books and articles, I often found myself admiring the analysis of what is and what was, but somewhat dissatisfied with the projections into the future. That was where most attempts fell short, in the inability to see the future in a way different than the way they saw the present and the past.

In a very real sense, futurists are helping us to see that we are into a major paradigm shift, perhaps the most extensive since the industrial revolution. However, while many people use the term "paradigm shift," the real implication of it is often either missed or ignored. A paradigm shift is not simply a case of ongoing *linear* change. It is not premised on a continuation of what now is, but rather on discontinuity with present and past. So, if we are looking at religious life in the 21st century, we need to pay more attention to the actual paradigm shift that is already well underway.

So, thinking of this book, that was the major direction my mind was pursuing. If we are into a major paradigm shift, what are the implications for the coming age of religious life? If we cannot think in a linear modality, then how do we think? What are the discontinuities that have to be considered seriously if we want to design religious life in a way that recognizes the impact of this major shift?

Then I read Numbers that early weekday morning, and just as suddenly a very important second, yet primary, consideration came into play. It was certainly true that there was a failure on the part of the Israelites to perceive the immense change that was taking place in their world.

They were on the edge of a wonderful gift, the land of Canaan, a land "flowing with milk and honey," which God had promised them. They had just come out of many years as slaves in Egypt, under the domination of a powerful ruler. The scouts went ahead and for forty days searched the land, spied on the towns and the people. When they came back, they told Moses that it was indeed a wonderful land, but that the people were "giants" and the cities "fortified." Whether their perceptions were accurate or not was not the critical point. Their predictions of the future—a new slavery or being destroyed by the people of Canaan—may have been more accurate, based on their analysis of the situation.

Only two of the scouts, Caleb and Joshua, spoke out in favor of going into the land of Canaan. They alone claimed that they would conquer the land and the people, using the strange statement that "they are but food for us." Caleb and Joshua, like all of the scouts, were princes of their tribes, with proven leadership experience. They had seen the same land and people that the other scouts did; then what was the basis of their call to go forward? Not a different experience of the land and people of Canaan. No. It was their perception that was different. Not their perception of the land and the people, but of how they would conquer them. They reminded the people that "the Most High is with us" and that if God was pleased with them, the land would be delivered to them, as promised. What distinguished Caleb and Joshua from the rest of the scouts was their implicit trust in God, in the promise made to the people of Israel. They recognized that there had been a paradigm shift.

The very chilling impact of the reading that morning in church, for me, was not the story up to this point. It was what one knew would happen. What was chilling was that suddenly I knew—again, and for the first time—why it took the Israelites forty years to go from Egypt to Canaan. I knew, not with my mind, but with my heart. I wondered just how many times I had read or heard those passages and not been touched by them in this way.

Angered by the people's unfaithfulness once again, by their lack of trust, God condemned them to what they asked for: to not go into the land they feared, but rather "Here in the desert your dead bodies will fall." None of those "over twenty years of age" would ever go into the land of Canaan, except Caleb and Joshua, the two faithful scouts. They saw the same fearful things, they recognized the same dangers as the other scouts, but they believed in the promise of God, in the covenant, in the gift of the land of Canaan. They could accept that a major change had taken place so that their previous experience could not be the basis for the future. So for the forty days that the scouts took to reconnoitre the land and return from it in fear, God condemned the people to forty years of wandering in the desert, till that whole generation was gone.

The Future of Religious Life

As I walked home that morning, and for much of the rest of the day, I found myself returning to the full reading, and to the thoughts that it started for me in terms of the future of religious life, religious life in the 21st century.

So much of what we read and hear from religious today about the future is pessimistic. With great concentration on several realities, people talk of the declining numbers and the rising median age of religious; there is continual writing and discussion about the "vocation crisis." Often I find myself saying that the only certain thing that our age tells us is how many times Earth has gone around the sun since we made our entry onto it. It has little or nothing to say about what is really important, about who we are or what we can or may accomplish.

Numbers in religious communities have been a concern in the years since the "exodus" (interesting Biblical term) of members from religious communities began after Vatican

II. Yet, if we study the whole history of religious life, what is the aberration is not that the numbers have been declining, but that there was such an explosion of numbers in the middle of the 20th century. Historians (Hostie, 1972) have pointed out that such sudden peaks in numbers in religious life are often connected to major upheavals. Perhaps in the 21st century, looking back, historians will point to the three major upheavals (actually one three-part upheaval) of the First World War, the Great Depression, and the Second World War, as the major dislocation that spurred the high peak in numbers.

Our perceptions of the sociological realities around religious life may have blinded us to the more important aspect, that of faith in God, of trust in God's wisdom, and belief in God's promises. Years ago, when the liturgical changes were first occurring, and many people, including some bishops, were fearful of what would happen with the introduction of the vernacular, folk music, liturgical dance, etc., one of my brothers, an engineer, remarked to me, "The trouble with the bishops is they don't have enough faith. Jesus said the church would last till the end of time, and they are afraid that English in the Mass is going to destroy it." We seem again to be in a fearful time about religious life. The Quinn Commission, which investigated religious congregations in the 1980s, and the questions it raises, the various studies that have been done, all seem to be looking at the reasons why numbers have declined, wondering if religious life is coming to an end.

The Nygren-Ukeritis (1993) futures project looked at the various factors that may have had a negative effect on religious life: loss of public image, identity, etc. These may have had a negative effect, but they are not the whole story. We need to go back to the story of the Israelites again. The perceptions of the scouts of the anticipated difficulties may well have been accurate. The analysis of the authors of this study may also be correct; it is, however, not enough.

If religious life is going to continue into the future, it is going to depend on us, but it is also going to depend on our faithfulness to God. We need to refocus on the fact of religious life as one of the calls from God. We need to see it as the following, the discipleship, of Jesus Christ, through whom the new covenant has been made. The Israelites were challenged to go into the land of Canaan, even though they were fearful of the land and the people. Though they were just a ragtag mob of ex–slave nomads, they were asked to believe that God would deliver to them the land "flowing with milk and honey" and deliver it to them in spite of the Anakim, and the Amalekites, and the rest.

Religious need to have the same faith. We do not know what the future will be, but we do have some notions about what it might be. Like the Israelites, we sometimes find ourselves looking back through rosy glasses at the past, looking back to the flesh pots of Egypt. The poor Israelites began to yearn for their life in Egypt whenever the going was hard; they forgot that you cannot go back. They had a twofold perception of the land of Canaan; it was flowing with milk and honey, and peopled by fierce giants. Caleb and Joshua reminded them of God's promise, and also that God was not going to make the Anakim and the Amalekites go away. The people were going to have to conquer them, and that is what Caleb and Joshua were telling them, that they had to trust in God and then *create the future they wanted* by going in and taking the land, with God's promised help.

Non-Linear Futurizing

Futurizing, at certain times, is looking at what is and extending it forward—the linear approach. During a time of paradigm shift (which is certainly what the Israelites were experiencing), such linear thinking will not work, because the paradigm shift introduces discontinuity rather than continuity. It is the discontinuities that need to be the basis both for thinking and for acting when in a paradigm shift.

We need to see the present reality and the possible future in a way that is different from our usual linear viewpoint. We need as well to act in a way that assumes non-linearity. We have a part to play in terms of the coming of the new age in religious life and the church. One futurist, Dennis Gabor, said: "We can't really predict the future at all. All we can do is invent it" (Pohl, 1993). There are some indications of what the future *might* look like, based in some cases on linear progression and in other cases on an understanding of the paradigm shift in which we already live. God was giving the Israelites an invitation to invent a new future for themselves. God may be giving us the same chance now. It certainly looks that way.

Inventing Our Future

What this book is about is that twofold aspect: first, inventing a future for religious life that recognizes that we are no longer involved in linear change; and second, living out of a tremendous belief in God, trusting that if religious life still has something to offer the people of God, then it will be transformed and will continue. This takes both knowledge and faith. We need to *scout* the land of the future, and we need to have a faith deep enough and strong enough to walk into that land, fearful perhaps, but not daunted by our fear.

What if we give in to the fear? What if we decide that the flesh pots of Egypt are better? Suppose we decide that it is better to stay with what we know, which is really what we have been doing during much of the renewal of the past three decades? What if we decide that it is better to return to the tried and true elements of the past, and simply fix them up a bit? What if we do not trust that the future of religious life is also in the hands of God, not just our hands?

That was the sobering thought that filled me that morning after leaving the church. Perhaps, I thought, we are on the border of the land of Canaan. We've done a little tentative scouting of the land, but are still thinking back to the days of clarity of identity and purpose, public image, institutions, numbers, and many new members. Is it possible that God is saying to us to go into the land of Canaan, the land God promised us? Is it possible that because of median age, and lower numbers, and concern over identity and image, we might turn our back, *because of a lack of trust in God?* And what was God's answer to the Israelites? They did not have to go into the land; in fact, they were not permitted to go, but were to wander for forty years in the desert, until the unbelievers were dead. Who knows what forty years of wandering in the desert might be for religious of the present time?

What I am attempting to do in this book is to combine the two elements: a call for a deep trust in God, in our discipleship as followers of Jesus, with a sense that we can invent the future. In the coming chapters, I will look at some of the aspects of the paradigm shift, and apply them to a possibly desirable future for religious life, and to the faith demands that will be part of creating that new future.

It is important to look at what the various disciplines have to tell us about the future within the paradigm shift. This I will endeavor to do in the various chapters. It is equally, indeed more, important to place all of that within the framework of the call to be faithful, trusting, and to do so in an authentic response to the call upon which religious life is based. We are not simply people who carry out certain ministries, live and pray in particular ways. We are a people called. The call has always had within it uncertainties. At our best moments, we have been people of deep faith, have walked into the future with complete trust in God. We have not been afraid to use the sciences and technologies of our various ages. It is in the marriage of the two, knowledge and faith, that our future may lie. And if God is not in fact calling us to a future, if religious life has completed its task, which I don't believe, but am willing to consider, it is God who will tell us this. It is not for us to turn away from the land of Canaan.

CHAPTER I

The Paradigm Shifts

"A New Creation"

As we approach the millennium, the sense for a future that may be different is growing, both in popular thought and literature, and in the work of serious thinkers. The emergence of "doomsday" predictions, found in earlier millennial moments, reminds us of the fear and the superstition, as well as the religious concerns, connected to a thousandth year. At the same time, there is a feeling among many people, including many futurists, that this change is not related only to the date, but also to the fact that we are in the midst of a major paradigm shift. Increasingly people are calling attention to the fact that some of the changes being observed are *not* the next steps in a gradual evolution. Trends that for generations have continued and developed, but have been based on certain patterns, are being supplanted by completely new trends, rooted in a radical shift. Some of these have been apparent for years; others are only now coming to our attention. It is not so much that they are just now occurring, but rather that we are seeing them, in a sense, for the first time.

Since its beginnings, religious life has been situated within its own time and culture and been affected by it. In some eras, religious have attempted and been successful, more or less, at resisting elements of their own time and place. At other times, religious life has had a major influence on developments. What has seldom, if ever, happened has been a complete separation. Even when the early hermits fled from the corruption of the world into the desert, their very act was a response to the situation around them and influenced what they fled. Religious are a people of a time and a place, and they can have an influence, and they can be influenced. What is not possible is to be entirely unaffected.

Writers have been pointing to a variety of major shifts that have been going on for some time; the lists vary in length and specificity. What is startling is that there are so many commonalities on the various lists. Depending on the interest of the writer, some of the shifts get more attention than others.

This chapter will look at some of the major shifts that I believe will have an effect on religious life in the 21st century, or upon which religious life has an opportunity to have an effect.

Nature of Paradigm Shifts

It is important to distinguish, as I have noted, between linear change and paradigm shifts. Linear change is change based on continuation of what has been, with some variations. It is often what we mean when we talk about trends and how a particular trend may continue into the future. For paradigm shifts, there is a different reality. Thomas Kuhn, who introduced the concept of paradigm shift, defined it as that moment when the earlier system of belief is no longer working and a new one has begun to replace it, bringing with it new theories and new understandings of the underlying realities. He noted that these shifts in the political realm often mean "the partial relinquishment of one set of institutions in favor of another" and that ". . . as the crisis deepens, many . . . commit themselves to some concrete proposal for the reconstruction of society in a new institutional framework" (Kuhn, 1962, p. 92). One of the characteristics of a paradigm shift as compared with a simple trend change is that there is a significant and relatively sudden break with the past so that what follows is discontinuous with what went before.

Looking at the same concept of paradigm shift from the social and political view, Capra, Steindl-Rast, and Matus describe the shift as

a constellation of concepts, values, perceptions, and practices, shared by a community that forms a particular vision of reality that is the basis of the way the community organizes itself. It is necessary for a paradigm *to be shared by a community* [emphasis mine]. . . . When there are problems, which [Kuhn] calls anomalies, that can no longer be solved within the dominant paradigm, these shifts occur. . . .now we are in a situation in society where the social paradigm has reached its limitations. These limitations are the threat of nuclear war, the devastation of our natural environment, the persistence of poverty around the world—all these are very severe problems that can no longer be solved in the old paradigm (1991, pp. 34–35).

George Land (1994) speaking to the Catholic Health Association used the term "breakpoint" and did it "to describe a time of change in which old solutions no longer work because the rules have shifted 180 degrees from what we have always known." These breakpoints are equivalent to what Kuhn called paradigm shifts.

It may be important to state at the outset that I firmly believe in the future of religious life, in the sense of a form of a specially committed life within the Christian life. Religious life, as it has existed in its various forms during history, is a matter of call, of vocation, and is a work of God. There have been a number of major shifts in the form, the style, the works of religious over the centuries. The major change points, those that brought the emergence of whole new expressions of religious life, were related to paradigm shifts: The introduction of monasticism as a form came with the immense changes wrought by the movement of the so-called barbarians over all of Europe with the social, political, and cultural changes triggered by it; the emergence of the mendicants was closely connected to the development of cities in the early Middle Ages, with the movement of populations off the land and the emphasis on cottage industries and major trade changes; the development of the apostolic congregations occurred with the growth of exploration and colonization with its widespread dispersals of people and the educational and social needs that accompanied it.

The committed life has continued in spite of, and sometimes because of, those changes. It is unimportant whether a particular form or style remains. How well religious life itself continues, however, will be in the hands of religious themselves, insofar as they are aware of and willing to work with and within the new paradigms. The current paradigm shifts may have caused, more than we realized, the changes in form and style that came with Vatican II as religious made the effort to first adapt and then to move forward. If this is the case, then even greater change is coming and it will be necessary to respond creatively and organically to these changing paradigms.

Resistance to Change

In any age of major change, there is resistance. Change is not something that human beings, for the most part, find either easy or congenial. There is a level of comfort with what we know, like an old shoe, that makes it difficult to face change. However, what is very true about change is that it happens, with our consent or without it. History is filled with the stories of individuals and groups who have fought it vigorously; it is also filled with the success of those changes, despite the resistance. We have the freedom to resist; we have the freedom to change. We may be either the architects or the victims of change. Insofar as we have choices, we need to pay attention to the nature of the shifts that are underway and see what within religious life will be enhanced and what will be destroyed, what changes are of the essence and what are of accidentals, where religious life is being called or where it is being driven.

Obviously, not all change is good; nor is all resistance to change good. What religious need to do now and for the future is to look at what is the true *essence* of religious life, what are the paradigm shifts that are occurring, and how best we shape religious life for the future. Why such shaping? Because religious life exists for a reason, not just for itself. It exists as a part of God's plan for the carrying out of the mission of Jesus Christ. Those things that impede that mission need to be eliminated, and those things that assist in the mission need to be embraced.

In the ensuing chapters, I will look at these shifts from the aspect of the kind of future for committed life that they portend, and also to the impact that religious might have and could have in the world that is being shaped by these shifts.

As always, one must make choices, and I have chosen which of the present shifts to include and which to exclude. My selection has been made on the basis of those that in my opinion will have the most effect on religious life, or where I think that religious could have the most influence, especially through their life and mission.

The Major Paradigm Shifts

Thought

The first and major shift is that away from the mechanistic, rationalistic mode of thinking that has dominated human thought for several centuries. In the Renaissance and post-Renaissance world, the total belief in the power of human thought and action reigned supreme. During this period, science and a mechanistic scientific method held sway. The controlling idea has often been that in every aspect of life things could and would grow better because of the power of scientific thought. For centuries, much of this appeared to be supported, at least for Western civilization. Human thought and human invention seemed unlimited. I grew up as a child of the Great Depression, assured that if I studied hard and worked hard, life would be better for me and for others. In my family that seemed true. Education and hard work have led to success for my generation. Now, the sense that science can solve all things, that technology can make all things new, is less certain.

Within the scientific world the advent of quantum physics has been a very significant part of this thought shift that has put into question many of the beliefs, systems, and applications of the earlier mechanistic science, based on Newtonian physics. The revolution in physics (Capra, 1975) has had a much greater impact than is realized by non-physicists. Many of the technological advances of the last decades are a direct consequence of quantum physics. Outside of science, this thought shift has also moved in a direction that in multiple ways has given rise to a new, and quite different, emphasis on the spiritual over the material. Many of the developments in the area of holistic health, including the ability of the mind/soul to heal not only the psyche but also the body, have been a large part of this paradigm shift. What was seen initially as a fringe movement has become a part of the mainstream, documented by research as well as by personal stories. What was often looked upon as quirky *New Age* game-playing, has now entered the broader field of health and health care. People are learning how to control blood pressure, inflammatory disease, heart rates, pain, and a multitude of other *physical* conditions through the use of *mind/soul power* (Chopra, 1993). The power of intercessory prayer as a healer has now moved from the realm of faith to that of proof (Dossey, 1993).

This growing sense of the importance of the spirit is undoubtedly now a part of a major paradigm shift, one that replaces the shift that started the whole mechanistic scientific paradigm of the late Middle Ages (Capra, et al., 1991). It calls for a new way of thinking as well as a new way of acting. Schumacher (1977) was dealing with the thought shift when he wrote of the need for new maps, "maps of knowledge" and "maps of living."

Ecology and Technology
The past several decades have begun to place doubt on the efficacy of a solely rationalistic mode. Technology has done much to improve life in some ways, but has created new problems as well. The great hope of nuclear power of forty years ago has been overshadowed by the specter of unsafe nuclear waste. The rape of Earth and its species to satisfy one of those species is now beginning to send its bill. The warnings of the early ecologists were ignored or made light of. That is no longer the case. As our air is polluted, our waters made unsafe, the land itself being poisoned, many species becoming extinct, the future of the human species is also at risk. The vast increases of technology have led to an easier life for some, but also to a great deal of poverty and disaster for even more people.

The growing reality of poverty is connected to much of the technological development and the ecological disasters that are now surfacing. The 20th century, which was to be the harbinger of plenty for all, comes to its end with an increase in poverty in all parts of the world. Rather than the sense that things are constantly getting better, that our technological skills are making life better for all, the reality is that it is getting better for only a few. Even in the wealthy countries, the gap between rich and poor is growing, the middle class is disappearing, and the coming generations will have less than their parents did. It is no longer enough to study hard and work hard in order to "make it." The homeless include those who have worked hard all their lives, but who have lost all in the years of recession. Poverty affects both rural and urban people. Farmers have lost their farms partially because of the technology that has made super-farming more economical and has dealt a death blow to the family farm.

What is basic to working within the paradigm shift we are experiencing is not simply a denial of progress through technology; rather, it is a movement away from a belief in and a dependence on technology alone. Technology cannot provide, at least on a long-term basis, all the answers to all the problems that face our universe. At the same time, to deny the good that technology has done is also a useless approach. What is occurring in this part of the shift is a sense of the need to bring technology and ecology together, to depend not on one or the other, but to bring an integration of the two, dealing with the questions in a more organic way (Sine, 1991). By "ecology" I am not just speaking of parts of the environment, but the whole of it, including planet Earth, the universe, and all the species. What is becoming increasingly apparent is that to sacrifice one part of our universe for another is to eventually sacrifice the whole.

Multiculturalism

The world has become much smaller in many ways, aided by the technological and informational explosions of the past decades. Movement from place to place, knowledge about different parts of the world, wars that have led to increased refugee traffic, all have fueled a multiculturalism that can be found increasingly in large parts of the world.

The crossing of borders by ever-larger numbers of people has brought into question the very concept of the nation state, another by-product of the earlier mode of thought. When so many people want to or have to move beyond their own borders, and when efforts to slow the movement seem more fruitless, the possibility of another shift underway seems apparent. The sense that one was born and would live and die in one place or country has been replaced in this century with a recognition of the reality of vast people migrations. While the emphasis has been on the reasons—economic, political, religious—it is becoming increasingly apparent that there is more to this change. It is the paradigm itself that is shifting.

As more countries become multicultural, multi-ethnic, many of the earlier paradigms about nation begin to fade. The problems of the migration give rise to other thoughts, about a world that has become very small because of information flow. The action that occurs in Africa is seen simultaneously all around the world. The idea of integration of the new people by the imposition of language and culture norms, has been replaced with the valuing of diversity, the enrichment of a culture by the introduction of other cultures at the same time. The number of people who choose to live in a multicultural neighborhood rather than flee in the face of the influx of the new people gives a hint that more than the demographics are changing. There appears to be a shift in the sense that multiculturalism is seen not as a problem, but rather as a simple reality, and even as a new and rich possibility.

This is not to deny the difficulties that accompany this shift. Just as some people welcome multiculturalism, there are those who resist it in many ways. In some places, years of apparently peaceful co-existence of different cultures have been replaced by ethnic-based fighting. Yet, even within the experience of the ethnic violence, we heard Bosnian villagers mourn the loss of the generations of peaceful living together of Christians and Muslims, some-thing they had valued but lost for political reasons.

Family and Community

An area in which much change is apparent is in the con-cepts related to family. We often use the term, "decline of the family." Certainly what has been in serious decline is the mainly 20th-century concept of the *nuclear* family, that family constituted of working father, homemaking mother, and their children. The change in the family makeup has actually been going on much longer in the U.S. and in oth-er parts of the world. The family, historically, in most parts of the world, has really been an *extended* family, that is, its extension was into the clan or tribe in earlier ages. Even over the last several hundred years the family included a much extended concept of kinship. In the U.S. some of the pioneering westward of the 18th and 19th centuries started the change, as part of the family, usually the younger members, moved westward to explore and establish new homesteads as the eastern cities, and even the countryside, became too crowded. In the last decades, with the increase of divorce, the number of single-parent families has grown and with it some resulting difficulties: the care and social-ization of the children.

Feminism with its rejection of the oppression of women connected with certain aspects of the traditional family has contributed to some of the negative aspects of family change. It has, as well, contributed some of the positive changes in family life and structure, with the under-standing of the varieties of roles for both men and women, and even for children. What has not yet occurred is the so-cietal changes needed to make the evolving ideas of family more practicable. There are signs of emerging new forms of the extended family through neighborhood, church, and other outreaches to single-parent families. The sense of be-ing totally on one's own as a family is being replaced with a renewed sense of community, and a search for a variety of ways of experiencing it. Some of the experiments of the 1960s in communal living have opened the way to seeing the family as less nuclear and more organic, that is, extending in a natural way to groups in the surrounding communities of neighborhood, church, social, and professional.

What feminism has done as well is to give new credence to the emerging roles of women in many areas of life in addition to those within the family. Women have moved into the arts, the professions, politics, and in a more limited way into the church. The particular qualities that women bring to these fields, when they retain their feminine strengths, is bringing about significant changes. We are seeing new models of what it is to be woman, wife, mother, and this is having a major impact on the children growing up today. Feminism is also introducing a new sense of what it means to be man, husband, and father. Some of the yearning for the past is being replaced with a slowly growing understanding and acceptance of new forms of family life that are more communal and supportive without a lifeless stereotyping of men and women.

Power

Feminism is just one of the many areas where new empowerment of peoples has been taking place for many years. The Black movement, the civil rights movement, the Hispanic movement, as well as many others, have pointed the way to another major shift, the power shift.

This is perhaps one of the most significant shifts we are experiencing, one that is affecting one of the major paradigms of the past. The centrality of patriarchy, and matriarchy where it exists, as the basis for power and dominance is in serious decline. The shift that is underway now, empowering of many different people, has not yet developed to the point of a completely new paradigm of power, but is pointing to a renewed understanding of what power is and how it is to be exercised. Much of what we are seeing now is a shift from one dominant group to another dominant group. A time that clearly is coming will show us the way to move toward non-dominance, and collaborative and mutually supportive models that allow for diversity and foster the rights of all. The emphasis on collaborative models is a particular contribution that feminism offers to many areas of life and culture.

Patriarchy, and in the few places where it has held sway, matriarchy, are based on the idea that one has power over others because of being either male or female. The evolution of this concept goes back very far into human history, and has had many forms. While both patriarchy and matriarchy are the same reality, it is patriarchy that has been the major power model for thousands of years.

The new paradigm is characterized by two significant elements. The first is the decline of the concept that one has power because of one's gender, and the special place that gender has been given in the realm of family, society, politics, and religion. This is not simply a result of the emergence of feminism in the last few decades. The older paradigm has been in decline for generations, but often in very subtle ways. Movements of empowerment of women, of minorities of all types (for patriarchy also has a *social* ladder of top to bottom among people), the protection of children and the increasing emphasis on their rights, as well as the growth of numbers of women and minorities in government, the professions, the general work force, and in the community—all these are simply indicators of the change.

The second element of the shift is the emergence of the broader concept of community, and of a community of equals. This is seen in the development of multiple kinds of community to which people belong, by birth or by choice, and, increasingly, by the free decision to associate. The family as the main and, in some cases, only community has lost much of its power. People choose to be part of many different communities, religious, social, political, professional. In these choices, very often what is challenged is the patriarchal modality. The importance of community cannot be ignored. The community movements have within them the seed for major societal changes in all aspects of life.

Another piece of the power shift is the aging and graying of the Western and Northern world. The 20th century saw an immense increase in the life expectancies of men and women in many parts of the world. The shift that has not yet taken place is in the improved *quality* of life to accompany the extended quantity of years. So in the West and North we have aging populations that are becoming more dependent and consuming larger portions of the goods of the whole, without yet knowing how to extend their general health and thus their contributing years. Age becomes a problem rather than a blessing.

The shift of power to the East and the South, where the young are the majority, is being further facilitated by this reality. Those parts of the world have yet to work out how to empower their young, and not have them simply suffer greater impoverishment because of their lack of education and opportunities. In the East and the South, the fact of youth alone will not be of most importance. Just as aging is not only a negative aspect in those countries where it is increasing, so youth is not simply a positive one. However, the importance of the difference between the two major parts of the world cannot be overlooked. The predominance of youth in some parts of the world is both a blessing and a danger. It is a blessing because of the strength and the potential of countries with a majority of its people young. It is a danger if there is an insufficiency of what is needed to make the life and the power of the young a positive potential.

The power shift to the East and the South will have major repercussions throughout all aspects of the human family, and the political, economic, and social structures of the West and North, which have been dominant for many centuries. The challenge facing the East and South is to avoid the same pitfalls that affected the West and the North. At present, there is little indication that they are doing this.

Religious Experience

In an age that predicted the decline and even the death of religion, there is a shift going on that will have diverse effects. There is the startling growth of fundamentalism in religious expression, not just in American Christianity, but in other countries and religions. The strength of Islamic fundamentalism is being felt in Africa, in large areas of Asia and the Middle East, and even in the U.S. and parts of Europe. As mainline religions seem to have lost their hold on the minds and hearts of people, fundamentalists, especially the charismatic among them, have grown in their attractiveness. The challenge is to see what it is that is creating the attraction, rather than in simply condemning this movement. Something here is speaking to the hearts of people, and not all of it is bad. Two major populations in the U.S. Christian world are being wooed actively by fundamentalists: African Americans and Hispanics. One of the obvious attractions is the emphasis on community.

Beyond the reality of fundamentalism, there is a growing interest in religion, but in new ways, often dissociated from the traditional churches, with the exception of Islam, which is growing worldwide. Increasingly, the interest in religion is more connected to the inner life and personal belief systems and disconnected from the institutional forms of religion. Within Catholicism there is a growing reality that educated people do not find sufficient support from their parishes and dioceses in their search to make religion a significant part of life. A relatively new level of religious sophistication leaves these people much less willing to be the docile children of the past. The major challenge of the coming years might well be how to support adult Catholics who wish to be as adult in their religious lives as they are in their family and work lives.

This change is related very much to the movement from the mechanistic to the more spiritual in the thought shift. While there is a decline in many areas of traditional religions, and a breaking away from the structures of these religions, there is not a loss of the spiritual dimension. That fewer people, even Catholics, now attend church regularly is well documented. That there is a decline in spirituality is *not* well documented. Indeed, there is a significant body of literature that would indicate that an interest in the spiritual is on the rise at the same time that the older structures do not attract membership. It would be too simplistic to put all of the blame on the patriarchal nature of most religions of the world. What is probably more to the point is the emphasis in these religions on structures, rules, formalized prayer methods, at a time when the paradigm shift is clearly in the opposite direction, looking for greater spirituality, fewer rules, more response to the Spirit moving within and among the people.

The early church may provide a lesson that can help during the present paradigm shift; the *ekklesia* saw itself as different from the formality of Judaism with its emphasis on rites and rules. The new *community* of disciples had to struggle with these questions, but saw itself as those who followed the *way* of Jesus. That the church became involved in the structures and formalities of the imperial, patriarchal model in the 3rd century was a move away from the community concept, but that element has remained within the church over the centuries in a variety of forms. The growth of liberation theology in the latter part of the 20th century would seem to be a part of this major shift toward the church again as a community (Boff, 1985).

Knowledge Explosion

One benefit that technology has brought to the world is the explosion of knowledge. Through increasingly sophisticated modes of transportation, communication, information flow, and even entertainment, the world has become in one way more knowledgeable, and in another, less selective about that knowledge. Computers are making all kinds of information flow faster, easier, and more cheaply. The educational potential has barely been tapped. Already ethical and legal questions are being raised. In many arenas our ethical development is lagging behind our technological sophistication. The questions now being raised about our institutions—educational, health, political, economic, and social—are only the tip of the iceberg. To try to stop the technology is to play the ostrich; the alternative is still beyond us. This technological reality has the potential for destroying us or of making a new leap for humanity possible. Our vision has to be as large as our skill, and that is still lacking.

What is needed is a major breakthrough in the area of ethics, one that goes to the essence of the ethical as well as to the essence of the new knowledge and technology. Falling back on rules and regulations, failing to see the changing reality, closing one's eyes to the difficult questions—these are ways toward failure. Too many questions now being raised by the advent of creative developments in the field of medicine are being answered with the regulations of the past rather than by applying the deeper, more essential aspects of the ethical life to the emerging realities.

Paradigm Shifts and Religious Life

What does all this have to do with the future of religious life? A great deal. Over the past few decades since Vatican II, with the decline of numbers and the aging of religious in the U.S., the sense of the end of religious life as essential to the church has grown, though slowly. My belief is that the future of religious life has little to do with numbers or age. Religious life has only a few times been relatively large in any part of the world, and there is not much proof that being large has been of any particular help, except perhaps in providing low paid workers in our schools and hospitals.

My thesis is that religious life traditionally has been leaven, yeast. Anyone who has baked bread knows that a very small amount of yeast is used in relation to the flour and the other ingredients, but also knows that the bread will not rise without it. Religious will have an important though different function to play in the coming age; the paradigm shifts I have described will be an important part of what that future will look like.

Robert Theobold (1992) has called the 21st century "the compassionate era," defining it as living "with passion." Many of the elements that he speaks to in terms of this compassionate era are things that have spoken very deeply to religious in the past, and perhaps will speak to us in the future. He points out:

> The compassionate era is based on the belief that security comes from mutual understanding, support and partnerships. The basic step we must all take is to learn to enjoy diversity and to live within pluralistic systems. . . .Community is, in many ways, a state of mind. It exists whenever people are committed to each other and willing to work to achieve desirable goals (p. 164).

Religious, over our history from the earliest days, have had a solid belief in the values of community, of living and working together, of dedication to the mission of Jesus, of shared goals, of mutuality. We have known that we could accomplish much if we were willing to work together *and with others*. In the U.S. the major efforts of religious went to the areas of education, health, and social service, which eventually led to a major educational system and a very large health system, the largest private health system in the country. Those systems are now in jeopardy, for many reasons, mainly economic, and the creativity that brought them into existence needs to be focused again on the vision and the mission, and the new ways to bring it about.

The shifts that I have mentioned will have an effect on what religious can do and be in the future. The future that is ahead of us may not be the future we would prefer, left on our own.

What we need to do is to come back to the vision, come back to the mission, and look at them in the light of the world that is our real world. The "signs of the times" that Vatican II called us to may not be the same signs we thought we saw 25 years ago. Like the Israelites in the desert, we might prefer the comfortable flesh pots of Egypt, hard as they actually were. The future before us is partly of our making and partly not of our making. We need to look at it and move toward it, using all the dedication, creativity, knowledge, and humor that we can muster. The future is partly ours to create, and we must be about the creating. But we must also be about the trust in God, in one another, in the many good people who are looking ahead to create a world worthy of the creation of God.

One of the endless themes in the Scriptures is that of a people or a person being led where they would really rather not go. Moses back to Egypt, the Israelites into the land of Canaan, Jonah to Nineveh, Job through the crucible of suffering . . . and many others. If we are to have a place, as religious, in the world that is coming, in the 21st century, then we had better begin the work of dealing creatively, trustingly, and wholeheartedly with what is being served to us . . . by our world . . . and by our God.

In the coming chapters I will look at the various aspects of religious life as they are and will be affected by the paradigm shifts that are underway. In such an effort one is tempted to be a predictor. This is often what futurists attempt. Rather, I would see that our role is to *create* the kind of future that we might wish, given the reality of the paradigm shifts that are occurring. Is this a dangerous thing to try? Indeed! However, prediction is even more dangerous. We have not yet developed the skills of saying what will be, so it is best if we try to say what *could* be. That is what this book is about: the kind of future we can create for ourselves and for our world taking into account the emerging realities. To try to create that world is probably no more dangerous that a Marie of the Incarnation leaving France for the New World, or an Anna Dengel starting a group of women religious dedicated to professional medical care of women in Muslim countries, or a Cornelia Connelly reaching out to the education of poor girls. Religious life in its best moments has been risky and risk taking. At its weakest moments in history it has chosen the safe and the known path. That safe path may be the most dangerous of all at this time in the life of our planet.

A final word about change and what has changed in the decades since Vatican II. Many religious congregations have undergone massive changes over that time, changes of lifestyle, of ministry, of prayer, of governance. They have been very momentous changes, but they have not yet touched what is of the center of religious life. In a sense they have concentrated on the *what* of religious life: how we function, what we do, how we do it, how we run things, including ourselves. That is the inward change (Chittister, 1994) that we needed to accomplish because over the centuries so much had become encrusted with non-essentials. With a major paradigm shift it is no longer enough to change the what; we need to change the who (the identity) and the why (the essence). So this book is about who we can be, about a new identity, out of which will come new realities of many types that will, in fact, change many of the whats. It is important to realize that the changing of the who and the why will mean, though it seems contradictory to say it, that we are changing the outward part of our lives now, who we are in the world and in the church, and how we interact with that outer reality. In a philosophic sense, we are now moving away from changing the accidentals to changing the essentials. In fact, as we are changing the essentials the accidentals will change even more.

CHAPTER II

Mission:
The Focus of the Future

"As the Father sent me, so I send you."

For apostolic religious congregations, the central reality at the base of their founding has been mission. For a long time this focus was buried in an emphasis on vows and community life and on the internal life and reality of the congregations themselves. At certain stages of any congregation's life the internal emphasis can put at risk the centrality of mission. Every time a group returns to its founding charism, whether as part of a major renewal or as part of a General Chapter, there can be a rediscovery of this mission. This was one of the major insights of many groups during the post-Vatican II renewal chapters. To go back to the founding charism of the founders, for the apostolic groups, led directly back into the founding mission.

For many, this rediscovery has been a great awakening, especially in the case of older congregations where there had been considerable development of the ministries by which the mission was carried out. What was uncovered, sometimes, was that the original mission had been redefined, but without a conscious intent to do so. In some communities dedicated to education, for example, they found that the original intent had been to educate the poor. Over the years, for many sensible reasons at the time, the emphasis shifted to educating the middle class or the well-to-do, hoping they would be motivated to working with and for the poor. At the time of renewal, some communities affirmed the changed direction of their mission; others reaffirmed the original mission and began to work to return to that mission. Still others tried to keep the two realities in a creative tension, with varying success.

Mission and Ministry

One of the results of this experience was a recognition of the confusion between mission and ministry. By "mission" I refer to the major purpose of the founding and continuation of the group. Mission is their reason for being. It grows out of the corporate identity of the group, and out of the founding and ongoing charism. Essentially, it is the connection to the mission of Jesus Christ. It is that part of the mission of Jesus that is given to or taken on by the congregation. It is the *why* of the existence of a group, its *raison d'être*. It is the essential element of the identity of the group.

Ministry flows from the mission, in the sense that it is the way, the manner, the method used to enflesh that mission and move toward its fulfillment. It is concerned with the *how* of the congregation living out its mission; it is what they do. In some congregations the mission is defined in relation to the healing presence of Jesus. Their mission is located in the scriptural base of Jesus' healing and of his calling forth of healing. The ministries are how the group works for the accomplishment of the mission: through hospitals, home health care, clinics, psychological counseling, and other forms. The ministries are very important. If there is no how-to established, then the mission remains beautiful words in documents. However, the ministry *is not* the mission, and should not be confused with it. At times we hear mission defined as what we do. That is a confusion that fuels the conflict between essence and accidentals.

When such a confusion takes place, then the congregation, or some of its members, connect their identity and charism with the works of the group and especially with the institutions founded to carry out that work, rather than with the mission itself. Mission changes very little over the generations, but ministries vary from age to age as new needs or new methodologies arises. For many religious women involved in health care in the 19th century, the major focus was home health care. Later, those groups started small hospitals in response to the need. Today, many of those small efforts have grown into large health systems, major hospitals, and a variety of diverse modes of providing for the sick. The mission has remained the same: to be a part of the healing presence of Jesus in our world; the ministries have changed considerably.

Especially in health care, which in the late 20th century has become a major business endeavor, it is possible for religious to find themselves somewhat removed from their sense of their mission, but deeply immersed in the institutional form of the ministries they started in order to carry out that mission. In some areas of education, the original mission may have been completely overlaid by a quite different approach to ministries. DeThomasis (1992) calls attention to the fact that in redefining ourselves it is possible to completely lose the original mission in the redefining. Such redefining may be undertaken to justify the continuation of particular works or institutions. We may, for example, find ourselves talking of the materially poor and juxtaposing the lonely, who may be materially well off, but lack family support and love. So, we redefine what we mean by working with and for the poor, by redefining who are the poor we wish to serve.

The problem is not in the redefining of our mission. What is problematic is to do it by way of rationalization rather than by conscious, deliberate redefinition. Essentially, the mission of religious is a part of the mission of Jesus, and where we have to find our justification is in the mission of Jesus. If we now experience the reality of the elderly as neglected, unloved, uncared for, regardless of their financial status, then we need to address that as part of our mission, not redefine loneliness as poverty.

A second important question we need to address is the identification of our mission with the institutions developed to carry it out. We need to recognize that they are the strategies, not the mission itself. Just as we have to be able to shift our strategies in order to continue the mission, we have to be able to look at our institutions in terms of their ability to contribute to the forwarding of the mission. Not all institutions need to be continued, and not all need to be continued by religious.

Creating New Ministries

As religious who regularly get in touch with the charism of their founding period, and with the ongoing development of that charism over a period of time, we are called upon to look anew and creatively at our ministries. Vatican II called us to study the signs of the times and to make the necessary adaptations. That work was done very well in terms of the internal functioning of congregations: governance, formation, lifestyle, all redesigned to be more supportive of the life and mission of the congregation. The ministries often were simply accepted as being appropriate. We had invested much time, energy, and resources in the development of a particular way of carrying out the mission. We also invested a great deal of emotional energy and attachment to the specific modes. Our schools and hospitals were seen as beyond questioning. Yet, certain of our members began questioning, challenging, and eventually leaving some of these ministries.

In a time when religious congregations have fewer

members, with higher median ages, this flight from the institutions has been viewed as a betrayal, as "doing one's own thing." A polarization has developed in some congregations between those who still see the value of the institutional or traditional ministries, and those who are calling for new responses, new ministries. There are solid arguments for both sides of the question. What religious have to focus upon is the reality of the mission, and the appropriateness *now* of each particular ministry.

Traditionally, the church has looked to religious to be the people who both identify and respond to new needs and to unmet concerns. However, the church also has come to look to religious to provide the administration and personnel for Catholic institutions. At those rare times in our history when there were many religious, such as in the mid-20th century, it was possible for religious to do both. At other times, congregations have had to choose. It appears possible that the Spirit speaking through Vatican II is calling religious to a re-emphasis on responding to the unmet needs. Later, I will suggest some ways that the present institutional base can be continued while religious move into the area of unmet needs.

What is crucial at this time is for religious congregations to take a serious look at the nature of their mission, connected to the founding charism and as it expresses itself in the present and the future. Their identity as religious is tied in with their mission, not simply with their works or their institutions. When researchers tell us that there is a loss of identity for many religious, the answer is not in a re-establishment of certain externals: lifestyle, clothing, symbols, institutions. The way to rediscovery of identity, personal or corporate, is in terms of one's reason for being—one's mission. The corporate identity is based in the corporate mission, just as personal identity is based in personal purpose or meaning. When one has identified the mission, then the dangerous but necessary step into new

life is to evaluate the ministries in the light of that rediscovered mission.

One often hears, when discussions of vocations are underway, that the young are not so generous today, that
they are not willing to make sacrifices, and so forth. Yet,
when you are in touch with the young, as individuals instead of as a faceless class, you find an incredible pool of
generosity that is being played out in the Peace Corps and
Vista, for instance, and a wide variety of volunteer short-
and long-term commitments. Many of these experiences
are connected to religious congregations, such as the Jesuit
Volunteers. It is hard not to ask why religious life itself is
not attractive to these generous people. One response may
be that we are no longer seen as the people who are on the
cutting edge, but rather are viewed as people intimately
connected with maintaining the institutions of society, the
schools, the hospitals. Are we turning over the frontier
parts of our mission to our volunteer groups? This is only
one aspect of the vocation question. More will be done
with this question in a later chapter concerned with who
the religious in the coming age will be, and what that will
mean.

Emergence of Laity in Ministries

The ministries in which we engage need to be both intimately connected to our mission, but also part of the creative breakthrough that is needed. Religious need to
continuously evaluate ministries, as how-to's, in a twofold
way. One way is to ask if they are effective, quality ways of
serving and of living the mission. The second and more
difficult analysis is to ask if they need to be done by religious in general and by our congregation in particular.
An example: Religious women started to build Catholic
hospitals in the U.S. in the 19th century because they were
the only people with the education and skill to do this.
Today, if you attend a Catholic Health Association meeting

you will find that a large majority of the leaders in Catholic health care are lay people, well qualified and dedicated. Is the time coming for religious to turn the sponsorship of health care institutions over to the laity, so that they, the religious, can move into developing those areas of health care that need attention: home care, hospice for AIDS patients, parish health? Religious are particularly suited, by reason of their commitment and their base of support in a congregation, to be pioneers of the newer approaches, the responders to the new needs, the developers of alternative ways to meet needs. Many religious are already in these areas, but often as a small group released from the usual works of their congregations.

One of the aspects of the knowledge paradigm shift that is having an effect in the Catholic church is the change within the laity, especially the emergence of a highly educated and dedicated Catholic laity in the fields of education and health care, able and willing to carry on the normal institutional works of the church, as called for by Vatican II, in *Lumen Gentium* (Dogmatic Constitution on the Church [Abbott, 1966]). It may now be possible for religious to let go of these, and move into the areas where for many reasons the laity are not able to go at this time.

Religious in the 21st century then will be people who have a clear sense of the mission to which they are called, that part of the mission of Jesus which is theirs. Their dedication will be to that mission, with a great openness to a variety of ministries that will make it possible to move toward the accomplishment of the mission, in a way appropriate to the new compassionate age.

Working in God's World

This may bring into question, as well, something that for a number of years was a given of religious ministries: separation from the world. Just as religious in their internal community life were separate, so their institutions were often separate from and parallel to the public expressions of those same services. The Catholic schools existed parallel to the public schools, and in some cities, such as Philadelphia, were even across the street from the public school. This separation in the 19th century had a great deal to do with serving an immigrant population, and with providing a place where their faith would not be in jeopardy. One of the clear aspects of some of the paradigm shift that is going on is a greater emphasis on collaboration as opposed to either separation or competition. Calls for health care reform and educational reform often have within them the spoken or unspoken questioning of separate systems that compete, when the good of those served might indicate the need for working together.

For religious since Vatican II, in their own lifestyles and approaches to their mission, the emphasis has shifted away from separation and more toward immersion, being present in a variety of situations. This immersion is seen as a way to be present to people and approachable, able to be part of their lives, open to understanding them and being affected by them, and serving them in appropriate ways. Some of the most significant ministries religious have undertaken have come from the experience of being with people in their suffering. Whether in El Salvador, Harlem, or South Central Los Angeles, when you are part of the people in their suffering, you are more likely to work *with* them instead of *for* them. The ministries that emerge are more likely to meet their needs and be acceptable to them.

With this immersion a better sense develops of what people can do for themselves and of the manner in which they do it. Over the past thirty years the understanding of community development has moved from doing things for people to doing them with people. Neighborhood organizations, community action groups, groups with specific concerns and interests, all point to a mode of being with people in which religious may possess specific expertise, but may not be the leaders or decision makers. As religious, we need to rejoice in the growing sense of people, including the poor, who are willing to help themselves and one another, which is alive in many parts of the society in which we live and work.

The greater understanding of the lay vocation, within the Christian churches, is fueling this even further. Vatican II, in *Lumen Gentium,* clearly calls the laity to a serious commitment and involvement in the life and works of the church. Here the right and responsibility for the laity to be involved in the proclamation of the gospel, to the righting of institutional wrongs, and to bringing their competence to the works of the church are clearly delineated. As a result of this document and the discussions that have surrounded it since its publication, religious began asking themselves what was the special work of religious, if the laity were to be involved in all these areas of church work that were, formerly, mainly the arena of religious congregations. The vocation of the laity as part of the church and its works would seem to fit here very appropriately.

Alternative Approaches to Ministry
The question of the separate institutions of the church and the continuation of those institutions is not of primary importance here. The key question is whether or not, at this time and for the future, religious are best serving the church in the institutions. If there are now dedicated, educated laity who are willing to take on the works of the institutional services, religious can look beyond the institutional to other forms of service to which institutions cannot respond so easily. An obvious area, historically dear to the hearts of religious, is service to the poor. Many of our institutions, because of economic realities, are unable to serve the poor to any great extent. In the past, religious began alternative services to reach the poor. These became institutionalized. To again move toward al-

ternative services is already a part of many congregations. Some of the community outreaches, primary health care, adult literacy programs, and many others are happening because of the willingness of congregations to release some of their members to these works.

At some point in the future, these new efforts also may become institutionalized, or the current institutions may find ways to connect with these new efforts. Someone is needed to do the pioneering, and that is part of the history and charism of religious life. Alternative methods and ministries do not just happen because we see the need. It requires commitment, creativity, and risk-taking ability. In the past, many religious were able to do the new thing because of their numbers, or because of their ability to interest the laity in the financing of these new ventures. Funding of alternative ministries will require a new burst of ingenuity, which already exists in many groups.

Another necessity in terms of new ministries is to look to the public sector. This is especially important in terms of serving the poor, minorities, and oppressed people. If you are looking to see where the poor go to school, then you find yourself on the doorstep of the public school. The poor find their health care, for the most part, in public health clinics, city hospitals, and emergency rooms. For religious with the training and the willingness, to work in the public sector would mean an opportunity to bring their skill and dedication to the public services that are there for the poor, but that are often insensitive to the people they serve.

In some dioceses, for financial reasons, the inner-city Catholic schools are being closed. In the case of health care, some congregations have had to close urban hospitals because of the facility's inability to be self-supporting. In the public sector, the cities cannot close their inner-city schools or their public health facilities. These are places where it is often difficult to find people who have both the requisite skills and the psychological support to stay in these positions. In some cities, the newest and youngest teachers are placed in the most difficult schools, because the seniority system allows the more experienced teachers to move to more attractive schools in upper middle class or suburban districts. Religious have the skills and experience, as well as the support system within their congregations, to take on these ministries. They would be receiving professional salaries which could make it possible for congregations to carry on other alternative ministries that do not pay for themselves.

Multiculturalism and Ministry

Another area of paradigm shift in which some religious have had experience is with the great growth in multi-culturalism in our country. The continuing migration of peoples, the increases in numbers of refugees, call for a major response of assistance for these people. While the government often makes financial aid available, the caring outreach of people welcoming and assisting in other ways is missing. Indeed, at times there is a frightening upsurge of racism, even among good Catholics who feel threatened economically and culturally by the new immigrants. It becomes important for the church to speak out to and for these people, and to remind its own people of the immigrant heritage which is the reality of all Americans, and of the gospel call to love of neighbor. Religious, by their service, have been and can be an example to the rest of the church, as they were during the great immigration surge of the 19th century.

Politics and Ministry

Over the years, religious have increasingly been involved in discussing the root causes of many of the problems now facing our people. The reality of political power, which is often on the side of the well-to-do, needs to be again tapped for the poor and the oppressed. Political activity is often a cause of concern when religious become involved, and yet it is one of the central ways of bringing about the kind of change that will eliminate some of the causes of poverty and oppression. To provide alternate services will be necessary, probably always, but it does not substitute for changing those laws that penalize the poor further. Political activity can include registering and educating new voters, bringing pressure to bear on politicians and city/ state administrators, congressional representatives and senators. However, these are all the kinds of things that good citizens are supposed to do. It is possible that religious could serve in appointed positions within city and state governments that are responsible for services to the needy among our people.

There is always a level of fear connected in the Catholic mind about political, elected, office. We run the gamut of seeing these as basically corrupt and corrupting to viewing them as a means to personal aggrandizement. As such, these offices for many years were shunned by Catholics and barred to clergy and religious. It may be that if we are concerned deeply about justice for all people, then both lay and religious Catholics who are committed need to consider the route of elected offices. At present, for religious, this presents a canonical problem. However, the history of religious life is filled with things that we were not supposed to do and that eventually, through the acts of courageous people, have become an accepted part of religious service. The important point is that if we want to have a solid impact on law and policy, it may become necessary to consider elected positions for some religious.

Collaboration in Ministry
Religious in the 21st century probably will be a much smaller group of people. During the mid-20th century we had several decades of unusual growth in numbers. Then, as suddenly as it started, it ended. However, large num-

bers are not, and never have been, the key to success in religious involvements. In fact, religious have been able, traditionally, to do very large things with very small numbers. They have been able to do this because, in a variety of ways, religious have worked with others. This is an age where there are many groups working to bring about systemic change, to work for the alleviation of suffering. Religious need to become part of those groups, collaborating with them, as well as becoming initiators and organizers of such groups. What is missing, often, is the sense of working together, which can lead to unnecessary duplication.

A few years ago I spent some time in western Canada, visiting some of our sisters who were in the process of developing an inner-city, community-based primary health care outreach. One day we visited all the other groups who were working in the area. At the end of the day, I experienced two very different feelings. On the one hand, I was exhilarated by the number of dedicated people reaching out to help others. At the same time, I was frustrated by the unnecessary duplication of time, energy, personnel, and funds, because while they were all in friendly relationship to one another, there was no conscious or planned collaboration. Had there been, the people would have been served much better, and the limited resources used to greater effect. One thing we need to overcome, as Americans as well as religious, is the attitude that we each do it *alone*. Our strongly individualistic character affects not just each of us personally, but also the groups we establish. Even when we are not directly in competition, we have a long way to go to reach true collaboration.

Another aspect of the future ministries of religious could be directed to the non-institutional stance toward new needs as they emerge. The recent experience of the AIDS epidemic is a case in point. For many reasons, it took us a very long time to begin to respond creatively to this devastating disease. While part of it was based in homophobia, I believe more had to do with the reality of institution-based approaches to ministry. These are far less able to respond rapidly to a crisis. Religious could become a more mobile, rapidly deployable body of people, alert to new needs as they surface.

Technology and Ministry

Finally, a word about technology. There has been an absolute explosion in the area of technologies. Not all are good, some are actually harmful, and others are simply overly invasive. However, there is an appropriate use of technology without being controlled by it, and religious need to pay more attention to its uses. Computers, a few years ago, were looked upon as some kind of demon machines that would invade our lives and overly control us. They certainly have that potential, and as any earlier technology, need to be used ethically. However, many modern technologies also make very possible a way of serving that expands the potential of few people to serve many. Religious need to consciously look at the appropriate uses of technology, and at the inappropriate ones. This will be part of the challenge of the future, because it is unlikely that the technologies are going to go away. However, like the wheel, and the printing press, and the telephone, they can be used for good.

CHAPTER III

Community:
Ekklesia and Discipleship

"Love one another as I have loved you."

The original word used in the gospels for church was *ekklesia*, from the Greek which means the "community which is called forth." One of the major paradigm shifts taking place throughout the world has to do with community, and the sense of its value and need. In the 1960s, we saw this beginning in the flower children, the hippies, and the communes that emerged everywhere. What fueled much of that movement was the realization that one was not really an *individual* but rather a *person*. In that distinction was the base for community to be rediscovered. The rugged individualism of the 19th century took it for granted that we could do things on our own if we were only smart enough, strong enough, daring enough, rich enough. Personalism recognizes the uniqueness of each but also the basic interdependence which is the human condition, and more apparently now the cosmic condition. Not only do humans depend on one another, but all parts of our cosmos depend on one another. The ecological movement has shown us that interdependence, and the community we look at now is not simply a community of people, but a community of Earth and a community of the cosmos. That shift is having and will continue to have very drastic consequences for religious life in the future.

Years ago, as a high school student, I was on my way to meet some friends when I went past the parish convent. The sisters there had been my teachers and I still had some contact with them. I had known them mainly as the excellent teachers who had excited me about learning. That evening, as I walked past, I found myself thinking that it must be really wonderful to live with a group of people who shared your interests, your purpose in life. At the time I was hoping to go to medical school, and knew that I would want to be with some group that would work together. The word "community" was not a part of my vocabulary in those days. I knew very little about religious other than my experience of them as teachers. To this day I mark that evening insight as one of the starting points of my own religious vocation that was based in a value for living and working with others who shared a vision and a commitment (also words not in my vocabulary then).

The other part of my experience of those sisters, and of the other sisters I met in high school, was that their life together was very separate from anything that I knew. We were not encouraged to visit beyond the convent parlor, and that was so different from anything we experienced in our normal life that there was little interest in getting beyond that barrier. It was a working-class neighborhood, and often families helped the sisters out by sending them food. It never occurred to us that the sisters lived better than we did; in fact, knowing how little they were paid by the parish, families with children in the school felt an obligation to make up some of the difference in goods or services.

When I entered my own religious community, where

our formation program was on a large, old farm, with very simple and basic accommodations, what most excited me was its simplicity. We had very little, but we learned rapidly that it was not things that made for happiness. There were many rules and regulations surrounding our lives that I did not particularly appreciate. I realized eventually that much was a monastic overlay that had little to say to a modern group, founded in the 20th century, committed to health care work in the Third World. What spoke to me, beyond those rules and trappings, was the sense of a community of people all united by a purpose, a sense of mission, and trying to be authentic to a call.

Changes in Community Style

The renewal of the post-Vatican II years brought crashing down many of the structures of religious community life: the schedules, the uniformity of prayer, religious dress, formal gatherings of the community on a daily basis. They were exhilarating days that were opening us to be more with the people for whom and with whom we worked. We were able to visit families, friends, colleagues, patients. The formalized evening recreation gave way to many things. The stark simplicity of our lifestyle, clothes, furniture, space, gave way to a more humane style. What we gained in the more humane, however, was balanced by what we lost in some elements of our life together as community.

We gained a new and very important openness to others, and an immersion in the world in which we carried out our ministries. We went to meetings, attended conferences, no longer separated from our colleagues by clothing and rules. In a slow but subtle way, we began to move more toward the mores of the middle class, educated, consumer society to which our age, education, and professional status called us. Free to meet with our colleagues, we had opportunities for a new and often greater impact on their lives and on their approach to ministry, and they had the same opportunity in relation to us.

Our houses became not only more open to others, but more like the homes of our friends, families, and colleagues. Sometimes, our houses became better than the homes of those we served. Personal possessions first became a possibility, then a necessity, and by now for some, a problem.

At the same time that all this was occurring in religious congregations, the Latin American bishops were calling attention to the situation of the poor, to the realities of oppression. Many North American sisters and priests responded to the call, and the concept of "preferential option for the poor" entered our vocabulary, bringing with it both a challenge and a burden. It is the rare document of a religious congregation today that does not speak of "option for the poor" and "simple lifestyle." It is also rare that there is a strong and clear movement from the words to the reality. It is in this area that we often find ourselves redefining "the poor" and grappling with what a "simple lifestyle" means. We know that it cannot be worked out in numbers of possessions or money; we also know that it cannot be lived without some pain.

We have experienced, as well, some wonderful new community realities, often connected to new ventures in ministry. Where once we would have worked in our basic educational and health institutions, and lived in large groups in or near where we worked, we now find sisters living in smaller groups in or near ministries that need or can support fewer people. While, early in renewal, we were opting for smaller groups because of psychological or sociological theory about small groups being more workable or more humane, groups now are small because the ministry calls for it. We have sisters living in ordinary housing in the neighborhoods where they work. They live with and like their neighbors, and become "good neighbors" in the sense of participating in the organizations of their area. Over and above the ministry, they are engaged in a ministry of presence in the neighborhood or parish.

Frequently the best things that happen in the history of religious life begin from a necessity and a response, and only later have the theoretical elements been articulated. Religious historically have responded to a need, done what seemed best, and only later reflected on what it meant. I "rediscovered" city and neighborhood, and with it a new understanding of community, by offering to take care of an elderly aunt for a few weeks. After over 20 years of living in separation from "the world" or in the housing connected to institutions, I discovered again what it was like to be with ordinary people, to talk to neighbors, to listen to the problems of people, not as a professional, but as one of the neighbors.

When I began to reflect on the experience, I uncovered a new understanding of community, but also of discipleship and of religious life. The vows began to mean something more real. Poverty was now related more to sharing of time and energy, of self, of things, rather than just not having things or worse, having them, but with permission. Chastity spoke more to being available in a loving way, open to the relationships that multiple communities called forth. Obedience began to come alive for the first time as a response, to God, to others, to call. Over the following years, several cities, and a number of neighborhoods, I have discovered a different sense of what it means to "love your neighbor" and to "love one another as I have loved you."

New Understanding of Community

What does this say about religious life in the 21st century? Given our decreasing numbers, and the possibility of transferring some if not all of our institutional commitments to a dedicated laity, it says that if we move into new understandings of the ministries that support our mission, we also need to move into a new understanding of community, and with it of religious lifestyle. What might that look like? Probably not the local convent of my high school evening walk, nor the old farm of my early years in religious life, nor the "sisters' quarters" of the hospital in Pakistan. We already are seeing some of the signs of the future in the present: in sisters who live in houses or apartments in the neighborhood where they work; in religious who "retire" to the subsidized housing for the elderly where they continue to be involved with and among the elderly poor; in women who live in small towns and rural areas, driving around the countryside bringing home health care to the people who cannot make it to the hospital or clinic; in religious in high rise inner-city housing who are part of the people, living and suffering with them, bringing their skills to the aid of their neighbors; in homes for babies who are HIV positive or who have AIDS; and in hospices for those dying of the disease, where the sisters not only work, but live there or nearby.

These are *small* efforts by few people, but they can have a ripple effect that eventually encompasses more people. Others in the neighborhood can be encouraged and assisted in their work of making their lives and the lives of their families better. What we learn from these efforts is that if you are going to live and work in poor areas or working-class areas, you cannot live differently from your neighbors. You bring your knowledge and your skills and your presence, but it has to be a presence that speaks somehow of the religious commitment you have made; it must speak to the presence of Jesus in your life. From being very good professionals in education or health care or other fields, we have to become as well good professional Christians, committed to the mission of Jesus in our life as well as in our work.

This does not call us to destitution, which is an evil we want to eliminate from the lives of all people. Like the

World Council of Churches' call, we need to "live simply that others may simply live." It is to live counterculturally in a consumer society that places great value on possessions. One of the messages that such a community can send is that sharing is important. Often it will be more a sharing of time, of energy, of concern, of knowledge, rather than things or money.

We are living in a time in the United States when people are calling for an end to the dominance of crime and drugs in their neighborhoods. We see startling examples of ordinary people taking back their streets. Gradually, the churches are becoming part of the movement, though very few were initiators of it. We as religious women can be a part of that effort, and we need to be part of the neighborhood, not separate and apart, to be able to do it. People no longer appreciate the outside expert who drives into the neighborhood in the morning and home to the suburbs at night. Being in community in a neighborhood means experiencing what all experience: the noise, the fear, the dirt, the discomfort—as well as the joys of children playing, of neighbors talking, of block parties, and community street cleaning.

What is key in all of this is an understanding that there needs to be a more direct and obvious connection between mission, ministry, and community. Community can no longer be the sisters living in isolation and coming out to do their good work. It has to become the broader reality of the Christian community immersed in, affecting, and being affected by the other communities around it. It means becoming one community of people who care.

Multicultural Communities

It also means becoming a community that is multicultural and unified in its diversity. Many 19th-century religious worked specifically with one ethnic group, and there are some congregations we still identify as Italian or Polish or

Irish. The understandable ethnic separation of the 19th and 20th centuries will not be possible in the 21st century. With the paradigm shifts connected with immigration, technology, trade agreements, and political changes, the nationalism of the past is taking second place to the internationalism of the coming age. In many parts of the United States, especially in our major cities, the mix is already a reality. Unfortunately, sometimes it is accompanied by racism as new social and economic threats are perceived.

Religious can be an active part of the new multiculturalism, and can begin to show it in their own makeup. Multicultural vocations will not occur until religious demonstrate an ability to get beyond their own ethnic roots and their congregation's ethnicity. This will happen first in a multicultural immersion in ministry, and only later in vocations. In the past, many people were attracted to a congregation because of their contacts with the sisters. I was asked once if there would be a negative effect upon vocations because so many sisters were working with the poor, with minorities, with ethnically different people. I took the question to mean that we were no longer in touch with the middle-class white populations of the past who entered religious life. My response was that it would depend on what we communicated to those young women in those areas, whether they perceived, as I and my friends in school did, if we would be welcomed to the congregation.

Community is a powerful attraction. Often, people consciously choose to move into neighborhoods because they see a community there, and they want to be part of an organized, caring community. They often flee neighborhoods where community has broken down, where the impression is that each family is on its own. The same can be said of religious communities. We need to examine our community life in terms of how we are living out our discipleship of Jesus, how we are being loving and caring groups, within ourselves, but also to what extent and how our community reaches out to and is part of the greater community around us.

Local Religious Community

In my work I find that there are many local religious communities that are in trouble. There are a number of reasons for the dysfunction. In some cases, there are people in those communities who never should have entered or stayed in religious life, and they are unhappy but unable to leave. Others were socialized to an earlier form of religious life and have been unable to make the adjustment to the life as it is lived today. In other cases, people have adjusted very well to the middle-class comfortable life that came after renewal and have compartmentalized it separately from their sense of themselves as religious. They live well and resist anything that will jeopardize their comfort. Often these are the people who resist efforts toward faith sharing, toward opening the community to others, toward involvements beyond the working hours of the normal ministry. While much has been written and said about community life, it has on the whole been much too superficial.

Recently I heard someone speak about "balancing our privacy needs in community with the mission and ministry." It took me a few moments to realize how strange that sounded, as if privacy and mission were on the same level and of the same importance! Or perhaps what I sensed was an assumption about community that said privacy was, in fact, more important than the mission. What is needed is a look at what community is supposed to be and to be about. If ministry is the how of carrying out our mission, then community is the people through whom it takes place. This means that community cannot be defined simplistically. Community is not only the people who share a common facility or house. It is not a gathering of those who work in the same institution or ministry. It has little or nothing to do with walls and roofs, or space at all. Community means people who have a *call* to share a vision and are willing to make the efforts to bring the vision to reality. My high school intuition about the sisters in that convent was not related to where or how they lived, but that they were involved in a shared belief and vision.

You can have an institution that does fine work, or live in a neighborhood which is clean and safe, or a house where all things work smoothly and comfortably. None of that by itself is community. Community requires that shared vision and the willingness to make that vision work. We tend to think of whole congregations as having a vision, and we name it their mission. We have vision statements and mission statements for institutions. If the people who are part of the congregations and the institutions and ministries are to become a community, it means a commitment to the vision that goes beyond words and beyond comfort. Recently, I heard a homilist say that the only command that Jesus gave was to "love one another as I have loved you." That was a call beyond loving your neighbor as yourself. To know how Jesus loved, you have to immerse yourself in the gospels, where Jesus lived and worked and walked and healed within the community that grew around him and to which he constantly reached out in invitation to join him.

We are now witnessing the emergence of the "intentional community" movement. I would hold that unless it is intentional, it probably is not community. By "intentional" I mean consciously answering the call by choosing to be a people who are in union with one another in search of and in pursuit of the vision that will unite the mission and the ministry and the living together. If we say our goal is to be a presence in a place, then we need to define what would create that presence, and what we have to do to become that presence. Too often, faced with the hard questions, we take the easy path and set up structures that will create community: organization, prayer, faith sharing, budgets. What creates community is the people and their commitment. If you are committed to something important, then the incidentals fall into their proper place. Community comes out of caring, but caring cannot be legislated. Caring is at the heart: caring about the vision, caring about the people who share and are working toward the vision, and caring about the people who are part of the vision.

Mission, Ministry, and Community

That is what the 21st century is going to be calling us toward: an integration of a true mission, the ministries that will lead to it, and the caring communities of people who are united by the vision and willing to commit the time, the energy, the suffering, the joy. It will be a community that lives simply, because anything else would get in the way of the vision. As in the old monastic communities, the non-essentials were legislated out of the life, so in the new religious life the non-essentials will be abandoned because they get in the way of the vision. Then we will not be talking about what things we should have or should not have, but rather which things will make it possible to really live the vision and carry out the ministries in a loving community. It may require computers and phones and cars—or it may not. The essential question is not the things but their value in accomplishing the whole.

The age of compassion will call us to taking off our blinders and looking with clarity, understanding deeply, and acting with passion. It will demand that we put aside ideology and rationalizations and live in the cool, clear air of the gospel of Jesus. It will call us to a community that is both larger and smaller than we know now, a community of believers, a community of committed people, who are not afraid of the unknown, or if afraid, go forward anyway.

It will call us to be members of multiple communities of varying intensities. If we have problems now balancing mission and privacy, then it will be even more difficult in the future. The many communities of which we will be part will make demands as well as contribute to our well being. Recently, I found myself listing the varied communities in which I am involved: my congregation and its various governmental groupings, my house, several other houses nearby that form an extended community, our neighborhood, our street, the parish, friends. Then I added the temporary communities constituted by the various client groups with whom I work. Then there is the family, adult siblings and their families. I stopped to wonder at the richness of that conglomerate, and the points where the communities intersect, what I receive from them and what I try to contribute. Privacy becomes a meaningless term in the face of the wealth of community as gift.

Each religious or congregation needs to discover or rediscover what will make this passionate, dedicated community possible. For a certainty, it will require plunging deeply and personally into the discipleship of Jesus, of walking the Jesus way, of doing and being the loving persons he invites us to become. "By this shall people know you are my disciples, that you love one another." And that love is "as I have loved you." Then and only then will we truly be a community, with all the richness, the beauty, the demands that make it up.

CHAPTER IV

The Committed

"Come, follow me."

One of the fears I often find in the religious groups with whom I work is the question of whether their congregations will endure into the future. In a sense, what they are wondering is if in the coming age there will be any to leave the plow and respond to the invitation of Jesus to "Come, follow me." If we are asking if there will be those who will follow the same reality we followed, it is hard to say. If we look back over the long history of religious life in the church, from the widows, virgins, deaconesses, through to the present day, then I suspect we know in our hearts that as long as the invitation is offered, there will be those who will accept the invitation to follow Jesus. What is not at all sure, and never has been, is that the mode of following will always be the same. The following of Jesus, discipleship, this will continue.

When I was a novice, our novice mistress had a standard assignment for all in her class on religious life. She took the popular name of our community, Medical Mission Sisters, and had us write essays on the three terms. My recollection, which very well may be faulty after all these years, is that the essays that were *right* were the ones that put Sisters as the most important of the three words. I don't remember what I put, or what I even thought at that time, except that it was very clearly the medical and the missionary aspects that had attracted me to this congregation rather than to those who taught me. However, without a doubt at that time, especially as novices, we were much more likely to see *religious* as the key element with medical and missionary vying for second place. Some would say that the religious—vows, spirituality, community—are the major and most important aspects.

Religious life as we have known it and experienced it, the specifics of individual congregations or even of families of congregations, may or may not continue into the future. Again, it is important to focus on what is the essence of committed life, of discipleship, rather than on the many elements we have associated with religious life in its many forms over the centuries.

This is not to say that spirituality, vows, community, and many other institutions are unimportant. Quite the contrary, they are very important, though they too have shifted considerably over the past years in terms of what they mean and how we live them. The core of the discussion comes back to identity, personal and corporate, and the founding and enduring vision that gives life and strength to the group. The vows, though we are in the process of redefining them, can give stability and power to our commitment. Without a deep spirituality it is not possible to continue to invest oneself in the mission, but the spirituality is not a monastic one, nor is it a development of one's inner life just for oneself. Rather, we are dealing in *apostolic spirituality*, which focuses on mission and gives as the theological base a deeply personal relationship with Jesus, an essential element to being involved in his mission.

Those who respond to the call in the future may find a different reality than the one many present religious met when they crossed the threshold of their congregations. These present-day religious may live to see quite a different form. I would like to focus on just a few of the ways I believe it will be different. "It" is the committed life in the church we now call "religious life" but which we may call something else in the future. The important thing is that it will be a committed life responding to the call "Come, follow me."

Community for Mission

This brings us back to the early church, to the original idea of community as a gathering of the followers of Jesus who met to pray, to celebrate Eucharist, to care for one another spiritually and physically, and to spread the good news of the gospel. A community that sees itself as solely or even primarily established for the welfare of the those who make it up can become an obstacle to spiritual development and to fostering the mission of Jesus. Community for mission and community in mission restores the intrinsically ecclesial nature of the concept.

In the early days of renewal, as religious were becoming more involved with parish, family, friends, and working colleagues, the complaint was often heard that we were living in a "boarding house." Community as a regular observance of times and activities all done together had died. For some of us it has been replaced by a very comfortable sorority/fraternity house where we have our own needs met so that we can go out somewhere to our work. This approach is being rejected by many religious because it confuses group living with a much deeper reality— community. When the two coincide it is a great blessing, but to consider that the group is the community is to miss the point of this very rich reality.

In one of the paradigm shifts that is occurring worldwide, we see an emphasis on the importance of meaning in life. There is a growing sense that who we are as people, as persons, as individuals, is less connected with what we do and how we do it; the connection is more with the *meaning* of our life, why we do what we do and live as we live. The shifts that go on in the professional world are clear examples. People who started in a profession, in business, or industry, often find themselves at a certain point questioning if there is any meaning in this for them. This is no longer a question of people dropping out. Rather, it is a sign of people opting in to meaningful lives, even if the meaning does not carry with it prestige and wealth.

The 1960s, the 1970s, and to a certain extent the 1980s were times of great emphasis on personal growth and development. The incredible explosion of workshops, seminars, new educational programs of these years were simply the tip of the iceberg. Gradually, people began to realize that even personal growth had to have meaning behind it. To become oneself just for the sake of doing so began to lose its value. It is not an accident that at the same time so many other movements were growing: human and animal rights, peace, ecology and the environment. These movements had within them already the seeds of a *meaning* movement.

This particular shift—the shift to an emphasis on meaning—can be the basis of significant changes in how religious life is led in the 21st century. Especially, it will affect who are the people who commit themselves, what they commit themselves to, and how they live it out. The concern about numbers and the aging of the current religious is to be unaware of the shift that is taking place. The responses to these concerns often focus on what we are doing wrong or why the young are no longer committed. There is no lack of commitment among people today. What is different is what they are willing to commit themselves to. I would hold that if religious life is going to be attractive to women and men in the future, it will be because the various congregations demonstrate a commitment to a meaningful mission that encompasses a diversity of ministries and a variety of modalities for being committed. The identity of religious will be more in the mission and much less in the structures of the past. What I believe will change very much in the 21st century is *who* will be religious and what it will mean to be religious.

Different Forms of Commitment

It seems quite clear that the religious of the future will include fewer core members, and will be older, committed to mission and to alternatives in ministry, less comfortable in terms of lifestyle, and more prophetic in the stances vis-à-vis both world and church. Indeed, we may find that what we are moving toward is more like our beginnings than our present. However, it is very probable that those small groups of core members will be surrounded by and associated with many other people who will be attracted to the mission, but who will see themselves committed for a shorter time, or even if for life, committed to the mission, but not necessarily to the institution of religious life, even as it is emerging and changing. What we may find is that we need to reclassify ourselves in the future in terms of committed life in the church, existing in a multitude of forms and styles, and integrated into a unified movement.

One thing already very noticeable is that relatively few people are entering into the traditional lifetime membership as religious. However, connected to this reduction in canonical membership, is a widespread development of various programs of associates and volunteers. These are men and women who find themselves attracted to a religious group, but with the desire to be part of the group in a different way. In some cases the attraction is to the ministries that are being carried on. In others it is to the spirituality of the group. Some are seeking a short-term commitment; a few are already asking for lifetime commitments to the mission but as associates. A lay movement that started many years ago, the Grail, has used a similar model from its beginning. It has always kept a small core membership of lifetime commitments, with a much larger group who associated with it for longer or shorter periods and in a variety of ways.

What religious need to look at in terms of the shift is the emphasis we have put on *time* and *form* as a basis for commitment. It is possible, as the Grail has demonstrated, to organize oneself with both lifelong and shorter commitments. The lay missioner movement has shown how people can commit for a few years, make major contributions to the core group and its mission, and then return to their ordinary life. What is also clear is that when they return to that life, they are no longer the people they were. The lifetime effects of the experience are noticeable, and the value to the church at large cannot be ignored. A monastic model may find time-limited commitments more difficult to incorporate. The apostolic model should not have that difficulty.

We need to look also at different forms existing together as a unified, committed life in the church. The one form we know presently is the canonical form built upon the blocks that are lifetime commitment, the evangelical counsels, and a form of governance of which all are part. Other forms could be based on parts of this, but not on the whole. In the past, there have been the Third Orders that were a form of committed life connected to canonical groups. New and creative approaches can be developed for this age that build on the response to the call lived out in a variety of ways. To move into the next age we need to be very open to a variety of ways to live the committed life.

In the early centuries of the church, prior to monasticism, there were many forms: widows and virgins living in their own homes and providing the gift of service to the community and involvement in community prayer; deacons and deaconesses providing more elaborate service in the local church; hermits of both sexes providing an example of total concentration on the contemplation of God; cenobitical communities combining the eremitical and the communal. The future may not bring back all of these earlier forms, but we have to open our minds again to the potential for new forms of committed life being lived out together, and recognize that it may be the future of religious life. Even now many religious experience different people and groups, who in their own ways are serving the mission of Jesus, but not labeling it in any way. My own belief is that some of the new forms are already here, all around us, but the difficulty is that we still look at a few forms and call only them religious life.

We need to be far more conscious of the number of people around us who are not called to the lifetime commitment to a celibate religious life as we have known it, but who are called to work toward the mission of Jesus. Religious are not the only people, not even the largest number of people who are responding to the challenge of Jesus to reach out to the poor, the sick, the hungry, the prisoner. Often, what these people most need is a way to connect. Religious congregations, beyond their short-term volunteer programs, could become a conduit and a support for these people. Associate programs are a first step, but it is possible that the future will see a more radical step, one that recognizes different forms of *membership*, including core members and other members with varied time commitments, single and married, men and women in the same congregation. These different forms of membership need clearly delineated areas of policy about responsibilities and rights, but also a recognition of an equality of commitment. While those rights and responsibilities may differ, the reality of a committed life will not differ.

Where the difficulties tend to occur is where we concentrate on the details of religious life as we know and experience it now: budgets, retirement funds, leadership roles, voting rights, and many more. What is worth noting is that none of these has to do in an essential way with religious life. They are simply the structural elements that we have developed over the years to facilitate smooth functioning. Many of the associate programs already in existence have dealt with these aspects with considerable success. Early associate programs in the 1970s were often made up primarily of "graduates," former religious who wished to maintain ties with the congregation, or to find a way to continue being involved in its mission. As these forms have developed and moved beyond the former members, the questions of funds, voting, and leadership are of less interest. The major questions are ones of strategies to make it possible for more people to be involved in the mission of the church, the mission of Jesus. Religious congregations could be one of the major modes for serious involvement of laity in that mission.

If religious life is still vital in the 21st century, the core members with a lifetime commitment, though fewer, will be able to move the mission forward through the ongoing collaboration of an increasingly growing body of people with varied time and form commitments. Religious, historically, have been joined by laity in the ministries, more in some than others. This will need to increase, but will be institutionalized in a way different from what we now know. These people will be far more interested in the mission and ministry, and much less interested in the internal matters of the congregations' core members, except insofar as it affects the mission.

Older Core Members

There is considerable evidence that religious life as a lifetime commitment is something that is now being considered at a later stage of life. Some Eastern religions see the commitment to a more spiritual life as something that is fitting only after one has completed the work of family and career. Those entering religious life today are older and likely to have completed their education and worked for some time in their chosen fields. This is related to another aspect of the paradigm shift that has to do with the fact that many people, especially in business and the professions, now tend to make a number of major shifts during their lives. Thus, the idea of starting in one field and staying in it till retirement has been replaced with the concept of numerous changes during life. For years, vocational counselors have been aware that multiple shifts of career are more the norm than the exception. Part of this has to do with the technological changes, and part with the increased information flow that makes multiple options and possibilities open to many people.

There are both positives and negatives of this shift toward older entrants to religious life. On the positive side, they may be better educated, more experienced, more mature. On the negative side, they may be more set in their ways, less adaptable. Among some of those who are even now considering religious life are the widowed and the divorced who bring with them a totally different reality than the celibate group they are joining. That can be an enrichment, but it can be a difficulty as well.

Religious sometimes place emphasis on the comfort of the known reality and fail to see the potential of these different candidates and what their different experiences of life can make possible in terms of ministry. Those who already have candidates and members from these groups can attest to the difficulties, but also to the values, to the varied experiences that can be enriching, not simply professional experience, but marriage and family experience. It may take some stretching for the traditional religious to understand the richness.

Multicultural Core Members
Another area of the paradigm shifts we have been ex-

periencing is helping to move the world away from separation and conflict: The Berlin wall came down, the communist empire collapsed. In a smaller, but very real way, people who emigrated to other countries have not entered into the melting pot mentality, but rather maintained their original cultural identity and merged it with the new. In the 19th century, immigrants to the United States wanted very much to become Americans. Now we see the emergence of African-Americans, Hispanic-Americans, Asian-Americans. This is not simply semantics. There is a multiculturalism, a one-world mentality that is growing and is a major part of the paradigm shift affecting all parts of life. At the same time, there are the movements countering this shift. So we find areas of terrible ethnic conflict which is looking back to a racial purity and continuously renewing the memory of past injustices. With each movement forward there are also movements backward.

Many religious congregations in the United States began as strongly ethnic groups: Polish, Italian, German, Irish. We had national parishes in many dioceses, and ethnic neighborhoods in many of our larger cities. The religious worked with the various ethnic groups. Thus, it was not surprising that most of their candidates would be from those same groups. One of the major paradigm shifts identified earlier was that of increased multiculturalism. The world we are in now is a multicultural one and it is clearly developing. Regardless of how people feel about it, and in spite of the racism and other "isms" that plague our society, the world will be even more integrated in a cultural way. The knowledge explosion, the greater migrations of peoples, as well as many conscious choices for diversity, are affecting society in general and religious congregations in particular.

Presently, the vocation promoter groups are spending a good deal of time discussing how to increase Hispanic or African-American vocations. I would suggest that the way vocations have come in the past is also the way they will come in the future. The people who join, either as core members or in some other form, are those with whom religious have worked, with whom they have lived perhaps in neighborhoods, with whom they have had professional relationships. The key question is *how* we have worked with or lived with ethnic groups. In the past, students in a school knew if the congregation was open to people from different ethnic groups. They knew it by how they were treated in the school. So today. If we work with African-Americans or Hispanics or Asians from a stance of racism, do-good-ism, condescendingly, the message is clear and unequivocal.

It is not enough to live and to work in a multicultural setting. How we live and work is what is very important. A few years ago some people began getting global citizen passports. They would not get you into or out of a country, but they did say something about a mentality that went beyond ethnic groups and national states. What is important in the multicultural world into which we are increasingly moving, is the multicultural attitude. This may be an area that will divide those congregations which move successfully into the new world that is emerging and those which do not. Multiculturalism as an attitude is based on a belief that in spite of our seeming differences, the human family is one (Harmer, 1993). The differences of language, culture, race, and mores are important and they are a source of richness, but they are not impassable barriers. At base, at our deepest level, we are all the same. We come out of a creation, and are part of a global world that is one in spite of wars, competition, and racism.

Our Christian heritage, the message of Jesus, has always been one of inclusivity. When we allowed our ethnic background, our socio-economic reality, even our religious heritage to be a source of separation, we have sinned against ourselves and our God. We are fully immersed, at present, in a world where diversity is seen by many as a problem rather than a potential. Even standing in a supermarket checkout line can be a trial as one listens to comments made about "them" by "us." The comments we hear are based in fear, and the fear expresses itself in contempt, sometimes hatred. This is of the old paradigm which is dying. How long it will take we cannot foretell, but that it is dying and being replaced by a global paradigm is clear and sure. It is this new paradigm of "globalness" and inclusivity that religious need to understand and embrace. To stay with the old paradigm is to choose death rather than life. To move with the new paradigm means that we have to deal honestly, creatively, and painfully with our own subtle prejudices, wherever they are and however they express themselves.

An Extended Reality

Earlier I indicated that we might be seeing in the future the reality of a smaller core membership, accompanied by a number of different forms in terms of commitment. If we are going to be a very small group of core, lifetime members, and other members who have different forms and lengths of time of commitment, then it means that we will have to *consciously* accept additional ways of extending our reality to accomplish the mission and carry out the important ministries. What is happening in the Christian churches and in many different religions, as one of the major paradigm shifts, is a growing interest in matters religious, often coupled with a distancing from the institutional expressions of religion. Many of the same issues are the concern of both religious and committed laity. In some cases the laity are ahead of religious; in others the religious are leading the way.

The proliferation of lay volunteer movements connected with religious congregations is a clear call that something very important is happening. These people, sometimes recent college graduates, at other times people in midlife who are free to pull back for a time from their normal career activities, are giving time to do something different with their lives. This is happening outside the religious realm also. The Peace Corps and similar programs continue to attract many people who want to do something that will help others and will give greater meaning to their own lives. Often, the people who enter them are changed, their lives are different, and their way of looking at whatever they do has been drastically altered.

In religious congregations many of the volunteers upon completion of their time make quite different decisions about the rest of their lives. In our Samaritan Lay Missioner Program we find that a few have entered our community or another; some become part of our associate program; others make career decisions that move them into lifetime service professions. This program places the volunteers with the neediest segments of our society: the homeless, AIDS patients, battered women and children, the economically poor. These people were attracted to our program because of the mission and service, and their lives afterwards are not the same. While some enter the program with the idea of giving one year to help others, many leave the program committed to a life of service, using a variety of means to do so.

In addition, there are numerous other groups who are working with and for the disadvantaged. If there is anything that is sure about the new paradigm that is emerging, it is that collaboration rather than competition is going to be the way of the future. The limits of our economic and political energies and assets would say that we cannot afford duplicate and competitive endeavors. Religious need to move out of a stance that says we do it ourselves or we "allow" others to help us, to one that says all of those who want to make a different world can work together in an immense variety of ways.

When we put a great emphasis on numbers, we usually are still in a modality that is speaking of numbers of canonical religious. These numbers are shrinking. If we look, rather, at numbers of committed and concerned people, those numbers are growing. When we look at collaborative modes, we are looking also at ways that the mission becomes the centrally important factor, and who is in charge, who is on top, who is running it, becomes far less important. Religious of the future may very well be playing major leadership roles in some of these endeavors and very minor roles in others. If the mission is being forwarded, that is what is important. For some religious it is going to require a major shift in thought. It is a shift that will recognize the talents of others, the leadership ability and skill of laity, and the necessity, at times, to take secondary roles where once we were the primary movers.

A word that has become very important in recent years is "networking." This computer-based term has come into common parlance as people recognized that not everyone needs to be in or doing everything. Many organizations and groups who would never see themselves as religious in any way are involved with some of the same people and issues as religious. The focus, once again, is on mission and ministry, even if those terms are not used. Religious have increased their ability to network with others, even when there are considerable differences of philosophy and even of ethics. We are moving into an age that recognizes differences and builds on commonalities. As we do this, we have to let go of our more rigid ideas and learn how to agree to disagree on some things as long as we agree on the important things upon which our collaboration is built.

To look at a religious life in the 21st century is to see a small pool of lifetime members immersed in a much larger group of committed people. The reality will need to be much more flexible and fluid than we knew when many of us entered religious life. The lengths and natures of commitment, the differing roles, rights, and responsibilities, will all call on us to stretch ourselves, our minds, our hearts. It may lack some of the present comfort of well known modes of life and work, of easily understood categories. It can be a very vibrant and challenging future, which will breathe new life into committed life and into the church itself. Over the centuries, religious life has taken on new forms, often at great cost but also with great rewards. I believe we are entering into that same major shift once again. What we have known will continue for some time into the future, but the real potential for life is in what is only now emerging.

CHAPTER V

New Place in the Church

"Who do you say I am?"

What can we say of the role of religious in the church of the 21st century, assuming the trend of fewer religious continues? A good argument could be made that the reduction of numbers and the strong emergence of the laity is, in fact, a life-saving reality for religious life itself. Since religious can no longer maintain the strong and exclusive role in the building and managing of the Catholic institutional systems, and since educated, dedicated laity are ready, increasingly, to take over, religious may be free now to do and to be what religious historically have been and done.

In most periods of history, religious have been very small in numbers within the total church, and yet they have made significant contributions. Over the long history of religious life, two roles have been appropriately the domain of religious: the prophetic and the pioneer. Both of these are appropriate to the religious life, but, I am convinced, both have been overshadowed by the staffing and maintenance roles of the recent past.

The Prophetic Role

During much of the 20th century, religious, especially women, were honored and cherished members of the church. Books were published referring to them as daughters of the church. The esteem they enjoyed did not always translate into either financial assistance or power in the church, but it gave them some subtle influence. The institutions they founded, especially schools and hospitals, were honored for their contributions. What also happened, however, was that an image of religious women developed that was far from the reality we ourselves knew. They were looked upon as docile daughters, obedient followers of pope and bishops and pastors. There was a fairly high degree of prestige connected to the family who had a daughter in the convent, though it was not as high, of course, as having a son a priest!

The reality of religious life for both men and women, throughout its history, has been that it has often been at cross purposes with the church and its leaders. Religious life, by its nature of reaching out to meet new needs and serve the uncherished, has at its best moments been prophetic and as a result often seen to be rebellious. Many of the ventures that eventually came to be honored began in conflict. The religious often were a thorn in the side of a bishop because of wishing to serve those who were neglected by the church or by society at large.

A good friend, an Episcopal priest, used to speak of religious as "the Protestants of the Catholic church." He said this as praise, in the sense that religious exercise their prophetic roles and challenge the church and the world as part of their nature.

While there may be some longing in the heart to have church leaders listen and respond positively to what religious are seeing, calling for, moving toward, it is not of the nature of either for such a thing to happen. The prophet must stand in challenge to the status quo; church leadership has a role in preserving (Brueggemann, 1983). It is the combination of these two, and their constant interactions, that keeps the church and religious true to their mission. If either capitulates too easily to the other, as has often happened in the history of religious congregations, the church is less for it. It is peace bought like a mess of potage in exchange for one's birthright. As religious, we need to be more at ease with the fact of non-acceptance and conflict. As long as we continue to love the *ekklesia* that Jesus founded, and work for the mission of Jesus, then all of these conflicts will help rather than harm in the long run. Of course, in the short run it is very frustrating and potentially alienating.

Once when I was working with a monastic community, during a time when people were asking themselves, "Are we not daughters of the church?" the group was having a major disagreement with the local bishop. Some of the older sisters were very concerned that this was not appropriate for religious. Then during a story-sharing session, going back many years because some of the women were in their eighties and nineties, one elderly member suddenly went up to the large newsprint pad and indicated a number of times when the monastery was in conflict with the bishop. Then she turned to the group and said, "We are a group who fights with bishops. And we have survived and so has the church." That could well be a motto for the coming years. The church will survive and so will we. I would suggest that we will all be the better for it.

When religious life is at its best and strongest, it is lovingly prophetic vis-à-vis church and world. That does not suggest that the conflict is not sometimes very acrimonious, on both sides. It is to propose rather that the role of prophecy is to challenge, and that is rarely a pleasant experience. It is wholesome, once in a while, to go back to the Hebrew Scriptures and read how prophets were treated, but also how the people eventually benefitted. Prophecy, for any society or institution, is essential for life and growth. What is important, I believe, is to stay the course. The temptation is to move out of and away from the conflict, either by compliance, collusion, or walking away. There is no doubt that many women in the church today are taking the third route of walking away, out of anger and alienation. Their decision is understandable and I am deeply in sympathy with them. For religious, I believe the answer is to stay with the conflict, stay with the alienation if needed, but also stay with the prophetic demand and its consequences.

The prophetic role of the religious can be traced over and over during the long history of religious life from its inception among the widows, virgins, and deaconesses of the earliest centuries until the present. This role has led to the religious in various ages calling attention, of the church or of the civil order, to the needs of the people of God. Sometimes the need was in their own area; in other cases it was to other parts of the world. It has been a key part of the religious charism to call to the attention of the church itself where it was failing in its service of the people of God. A Catherine of Siena or Teresa of Avila, a Dominic or Francis, were voices calling the church itself to be true to its nature.

The prophetic role is difficult while it is being exercised. Only later does history bless it and honor it. For many years, that prophetic voice has been very quiet, but it is once again being heard. To be prophet means to be a *conscience* of the group, which is not a popular activity, nor one that brings with it support, affirmation, or affection.

The Pioneer Role

The pioneer role of religious congregations has been there throughout the centuries as well. The central word in the pioneering roles has been *alternative*. It is in alternatives that religious have made, in the past, the contributions that eventually led to new systems and to major change. Alternative modes, usually starting small, take time to catch on, but they are the seeds of change that are so necessary. In the world of business and industry, alternatives are often developed and take their first step forward in the entrepreneurial world. The personal computer revolution was started by young hackers working in garages and basements, and in that realm they overtook and passed the giants in the industry. Religious, who often have been the entrepreneurs of the church, need to reaffirm this role, knowing that what they start may become, eventually, an institution or a system that can then be taken over and run by the laity, while the religious move on once again.

This is one of the ideas associated in the past with missionaries who were seen as people who were to work their way out of a job. The idea was to move into an area, start something, train the local people, and then *move on*. Missionaries have not always done that, but it was always a part of the charism. The Acts of the Apostles is filled with stories of the first generation coming to a place, preaching, baptizing, inviting the group to choose leaders, and then *moving on*. They did not wait long years to empower the new converts; they did it in a very short time. Religious, increasingly, need to incorporate this same sense. "To move on" means to realize that the response to the new needs is possible only if others have been trained and empowered to continue the church's work. Rather than being colonists, the religious are to be the *trailblazers* of the future. This is closer to the traditional role of religious than being the builders and maintainers of institutions.

Religious of the future have to be committed, deeply and completely, to the mission of Jesus and to the true community of the faithful people of God. That does not leave room for the warm and cozy life of honored daughters and sons of the church, nor for the comfort of a secure life. Rather, it means to be always on the move, always searching for the will of God and the needs of the people, especially the poor, the oppressed, the marginalized, the voices crying out. It means to be consciously and willingly responding to the challenge that Yahweh gave to Israel (Isaiah 58:6–7):

Is not this the fast that I choose:
to loose the bonds of injustice,
to undo the thongs of the yoke;
to let the oppressed go free,
and to break every yoke?
Is it not to share your bread with the hungry,
and bring the homeless poor into your house;
when you see the naked, to cover them,
and not to hide yourself from your own kin?

Religious life in the future will need to be inserted even more radically into the community of the people, bringing both baptismal and vowed dedication. We still hear people worrying that religious will lose their special character if they are too deeply involved in and with the laity. This is certainly true if religious take on the middle-class, professional role which many religious could, based on their education and experience. It would be true if they allowed themselves to be co-opted by the consumer society all around them. What they need to bring to this deep involvement with laity is the sense of the radical effect of being disciples of Jesus Christ, immersed in his mission.

This undoubtedly means giving up some of the prestige associated with much of the life in the past. The "good sisters" of the past may give way to the "troublesome sisters" of the future. To be prophetic, to be pioneer, is not necessarily or even likely to be favored by the powerful people of this world. As religious women gave up their special ways of dressing in the early days of renewal, they discovered that they lost some of the perks of being religious:

the discounts in the stores, the free rides on buses, the deference in lines. Strange perks for people dedicated to a vowed life of following Jesus! The religious of the 21st century will want to work in and with the church, but have already experienced the reality that they are not automatically in favor with the local ordinaries of the church they hope to serve.

The roles of prophet and pioneer can be undermined by a pride in the roles. The Greek dramatists warned of the dangers of *hubris*, the special pride of the hero, the one called to a special task who forgets that it is the gods who make all possible. To be prophet and pioneer means to be so in humility, i.e. in truth, recognizing that it is a gift and a demand being made, not a personal talent based in one's own gifts. To be prophet and pioneer also means to be so in love, not in anger or in arrogance. We need to take a page from the book of the great saints of nonviolence who sacrificed themselves for the goals they were trying to accomplish. This is very different from the self-serving gurus who garner fame and fortune from their roles.

New Approach to the Vows

Something that may need to change in the 21st century is the nature and understanding of the vows, the evangelical counsels (Schneiders, 1986). Since the Middle Ages the three vows have been poverty, chastity/celibacy, and obedience. Over the years of renewal there have been many redefinitions of the vows, and innumerable attempts to explain what they are and what they are not. A new approach to the vows is needed, one that will go beyond redefining words. It is too soon to say what the new vows will be, but already there are some hints of areas where they may emerge. The vows, to be life-giving, must capture the essence of what committed life is and the mission it is working toward.

Already we see considerable redefining of the vows, in

official documents such as constitutions, in records of Chapters, in published writings. A few of the present developments may be pointing toward the future. Most are elaborations of the present vows, but coming closer to the reality of how the vows are now understood and practiced.

Obedience

The vow of obedience is now less connected to questions of command and control, and is increasingly less focused on leaders. Rather obedience is discussed more in terms of the root concept underlying the word, *listening*. The one to whom one must listen, in a vowed obedience, is God, speaking to the person through the inner authority that exists in everyone, but also through the community, and through the charism, vision, and decisions made within each congregation. Such an understanding of obedience is based in the commitment that religious make to be responsible for the good of all, of accepting the will of God as it is expressed and lived out around us. It especially relates to the acceptance of the demands of mission and the personal costs of that mission. It requires a willingness to be in a discerning stance, a listening stance. It is a freeing vow in that when it is lived deeply it gives one the power to live in fidelity, in freedom, and in service.

Poverty

This vow is being redefined away from concepts of ownership and of use with permission. Much of what we used to list as the *spirit* of the vow as contrasted with the *legality* of the vow has become more central to the definition as vow. To live the vow of poverty is to live authentically, to live in a way that matches what we say about ourselves personally and corporately. It means to live in a way that is countercultural, that challenges what our society says is necessary for life and happiness. It places us on the way to defy materialism, consumerism, and the justified selfishness of "me-ism." Such a vow has less to do with ownership and more to do with stewardship, not owning things but caring for them and sharing them with all. It is part of the call to live simply so that others may simply live.

Poverty, however, is no longer just about things. Today it calls religious to share not only things, but also themselves, their time, their energy, their skills and talents. At its deepest level, the vow calls us back to a deep trust in God, living in the security of divine love rather than in the security of congregational assets, portfolios, and properties. In the coming age, religious congregations may have to learn to live in a totally different way than we have known and accepted almost without question. A real poverty will lead us into living more justly and more trustingly.

Celibacy

As we know it today, celibacy has more to do with being loving persons than in sacrificing our sexuality. The essential aspect is that the single-hearted love of God, which we have always said was most important, is leading us into a deeper understanding of what loving others means. It has to do with loving others without necessarily being loved in return, not limiting our love to community, family, friends, and like-minded people. It calls us to an encompassing love rather than to a restrictive one. It opens us, if we are unafraid, to the true passion of life.

Much of what is problematic in religious community life is engendered by the lack of true love. Love in the local living group, or in the extended community, is more than the "warm fuzzies," more than being nice and civilized toward one another, and it is immensely more than being tolerant of one another.

I was asked at a formation meeting recently, what it meant to be loving in community. My response listed what I believe one does when one loves another: One gives support in times of trial and difficulty, courage when trying the new, challenge and a call to accountability when we lose sight of the path or the goal. Love means caring, being just, being willing to walk the extra mile, giving of time and energy. Jesus gave us the measure of love when he said: "Love one another as I have loved you." This is what the vow of celibacy means today.

New vows may well be found in the areas of mission, of commitment to the people of God, of detachment from the goods of the world, of protection of all creation. At various points in history there have been groups who made one vow, that of obedience, with the sense that it included all else. Perhaps in the future we will make a vow of *living religiously for the sake of the mission*, with the understanding that the vow demands of us whatever is necessary. This would call us to continuing reflection, individually and as groups, on the nature of our commitment and its changing demands. What would not work, and has not worked for a long time, would be the simple and detailed listings of the shoulds and shouldn'ts of the vows.

Religious: Still Needed?

The immersion in the world of the laity, the elimination of the ideas of separation and specialness, does not assume that there will not be a role for religious in the church. Rather, it makes a greater demand on those who respond to the call. What will be gone will be the specialness in the sense of privilege and prestige. The specialness that will remain will be what has been a part of religious life at its best moments, a specialness of service and of commitment to the fuller and more all-encompassing response to the mission of Jesus. What may disappear as well may be the placement of religious somewhere between the clerical and the lay states. Intended to be a way of honoring the special role, it has too often become a way to put religious in the strange state of having great responsibilities and demands from both sides, without either the power and authority of the clerical, nor the freedom and independence of the lay. The specific role will have more to do with the *totality* of the commitment to the service of the mission.

The 21st century could look more like the 1st century, when the community of the followers of the Way was characterized by their unity, their proclaiming the message of the life, death, and resurrection of Jesus, and their love for one another. The early communities had people in roles, but they were *service* roles, whether prophet, teacher, server at table. The emergence of roles of power over the centuries following the Constantinian era, while historically understandable, increasingly looks less like the Way of Jesus as we look back now.

Roles in the Church

Whatever roles in the church are carried on by religious, they need to be service-centered, not power-centered. Power is needed in the church, as in any *human* organization, but it needs to be the power of Jesus, as in any *divine* organization. The disasters of the past in the church have been connected too often with the power of dominance over service. Servant leadership, the role Jesus took as he washed the disciples' feet, multiplied loaves and fishes for the hungry, cured the sick, is what will be essential in how religious function in the church of the future.

Religious today are being drawn more into the pastoral works of the church and into the pastoral works of society in general. Many of the new ministries are in this area. The dictionary gives many definitions of pastoral as related to sheep and their raising and care; it also defines it in terms of the spiritual needs of a people. From being involved in teaching, curing, organizing within the institutional base, many religious have been drawn, understandably, to the more spiritual works of mercy. Two dangers are inherent in this move: One is that we think that it is *only* the spiritual that matters. What the world around us increasingly is emphasizing is the *wholistic* reality, the importance of the integrated approach to the whole person, or the whole society. The religious of the 21st century, whatever their ministries, will need to be focusing on the *wholeness* of what they are and what they do, and what they hope to effect.

The second danger has to do with the responsible function of true power. Often religious congregations are warned that if they give up their institutions they will lose their power to effect change in education, health care, etc. This has both a true and a false side to it. There is no question that those who speak from the base of institutional power can exercise influence. However, it takes only a cursory study of the whole field of education or health care to know that the power is very slim outside the specific institutions. What religious need to do is to become very much more astute in terms of how and where power is exercised and where they can contribute to the good and responsible use of it. What we have learned over the last few decades is the immense power of nonviolence, of communities working together, of even one person with a good idea for which he or she is willing to risk life itself.

Religious, even as a small part of the church and the society, need to be able to exercise the power of ideas, of vision, of commitment, in a way that will benefit the people of God. The old models will not work much longer, but the new models will not surface within the church without the efforts of those who believe in the power of Jesus who said: "No one can take my life, but I can lay it down." This is not powerlessness, but the recognition of the true power that exists and how one uses it.

If the trend in terms of declining number of clergy continues, especially in the Western and Northern worlds, it is very possible that the roles of religious will encompass more of the clerical roles, with or without ordination. Already in many places religious are functioning as administrators of parishes. Should women be admitted to the diaconate and to the priesthood in the 21st century, many of those who come forward may be religious. When I attended the first Women's Ordination Conference, I was struck by two things. The first was the obvious desire of very many women to serve the church as priest. The second was more sobering: the apparent willingness to take on some of the same failings associated with the clerical state such as dominance and authoritarianism.

One of the other areas that will change in the future is the clerical role. It is shifting even now because of the declining numbers of clergy, and the necessity to involve others in the various tasks that have come to define priest in our world today. Just as religious and laity need to focus on what they bring to the mission of Jesus, so the clerical state needs to be reviewed in terms of the role of the clergy in that same mission.

If women, and especially religious women, enter the clerical world, I hope they bring to it some of the strengths they have developed as deeply connected to the laity, to the people of God. They may look and act differently than some of their male peers have in the past. If there is an argument for the ordination of women that is convincing to me, it is that women bring different gifts and skills that will add to the fullness of the clerical state and the service it renders within the church.

What is going to be very important for the future as religious give up their sense of prestige, privilege, and institutional power is that they not give up their ability to impact the church itself. Church leaders could, somewhat easily, decide that religious are part of the laity with no special roles to play, and that they need to be listened to hardly at all, as is too often the case with the laity. Just as it is important for the lay-run Catholic institutions to be recognized as part of the mission of the church, so it is important that the roles of religious be recognized in the same way. This recognition is not for the good of the religious, not a way of furthering privilege, but rather for the good of the mission and ministries they foster. The dedication of religious does not decrease because of changed ministries, lifestyles, governance models. Their dedication remains strong, their commitment continues, and their influence in the church, if denigrated, is a loss to the church and its mission.

To be women and men of the church is a baptism empowerment. The addition of a committed life, in the sense of religious life, means a deepening and broadening of that baptismal call. If more laity in a variety of ways enter into greater commitment, we may see it as a new gift in the church, rather than as a loss of the specialness of religious commitment. If religious can contribute to that development among the laity, we can be grateful.

CHAPTER VI

The Synod on Consecrated Life, and the Future

"When they arrived in Jerusalem they were welcomed."

Before the Synod

The Synod of Bishops which met in the autumn of 1994 was viewed by religious with a mixture of hope, disinterest, and mild skepticism. The early questionnaire, the *Lineamenta*, sent to many religious from the conferences of major superiors, created unease because of a concentration on negative issues. One of these, the "vocation crisis," had a slant that seemed to suggest that renewal was to blame. There was a confusion between mission and ministry, with mission viewed as the tasks religious carried out. Most disturbing of all was an assumption, running throughout the questions, that the monastic model, somewhat adapted, was still the normative model of religious life. The unique nature of the apostolic religious life as a *different* model was ignored.

The International Union of Superiors General gathered responses from around the world. What was very strong in the responses was a sense that religious life has changed drastically, and that while there was a decrease in numbers, the *vision and vitality* were there in abundance. Many of the issues, which would resurface in the Synod interventions, were already at the forefront of the responses. Among them: that religious life is different today and will continue to change; that women religious, especially, are not granted the control over their own lives and functioning that is taken for granted with men's congregations; that the central importance of mission needed to be emphasized; that the monastic model is not valid for apostolic religious; that there is a growing collaboration between religious and laity, but often a very problematic relationship between religious and bishops.

It was also apparent that women religious see the hierarchical model with its "obsolete and cumbersome structures, policies, attitudes and 'theologies' unsuited to a radically transformed world: a modern and post-modern world that often impacts the apostolic religious life in negative ways, but also a world that challenges to newness" (Letourneau, 1994, p. 10).

Responses also called for a recognition of the prophetic dimension of the apostolic religious life and the necessity for it to be reclaimed. The importance of community was highlighted, but a mode of community more akin to the early church and less to the later monastic models. The value of inculturation of the apostolic religious life in the young churches around the world was also a major focus of the responses, coming as they did from all over the world.

There was a call for an active representation of religious, and religious women in particular, at the Synod. The question of competence to speak to the reality of religious life today and for the future was at the base of this request. The call for representation was in terms of the preparatory documents as well as at the Synod itself.

Makeup of the Synod

One of the results of the preliminary work related to the *Lineamenta* was the inclusion of a small but significant group of religious in the Synod, as auditors and as experts. There were 71 auditors, most of them religious, and 20 experts, all of whom were permitted to speak to the Synod and be part of the small groups that met during the Synod and developed reports to the whole. No religious women were part of the formal decision body of the Synod. Some of the bishops at the Synod were members of religious congregations, so there were religious men among the deciders.

Doris Gottemoeller, R.S.M., an American auditor, in her update to LCWR referred to the atmosphere at the Synod as being "cordial and welcoming to the auditors" (1994). The first part of the Synod was filled with speeches (over 140 in the first week alone) on various aspects of religious life, of the relationships of religious with the church and the world, and of the challenges facing the Synod. While not all the speeches are available, through *Origins* published in the U.S. and *Religious Life Review* published in Dublin, Ireland, some of the major interventions point clearly to what became the key issues.

Main Issues

Prophetic Nature of Religious Life

Though the prophetic nature of the religious life was ignored in the *Lineamenta,* it was brought forward through the interventions. One of the strongest statements was made by Bishop Kevin Dowling, C.SS.R., of Rustenburg, South Africa, saying that consecrated men and women have a prophetic charism that must be expressed in an alternative way of living and relating, a gospel way.

This alternative should be manifested in a clear option for the poor, solidarity with the marginalized and exploited—for example, women and women's concerns—and persevering dedication to challenging and overcoming all forms of injustice and oppression (Dowling, 1994, p. 308).

Timothy Radcliffe, Master General of the Dominicans, noted the tendency to be fearful about the prophetic because of the element of challenge and debate.

Too often in the church we are afraid, afraid of debate. There is no need for fear. From the days of Pentecost, the church has known tensions. The community of Jerusalem, which was "one in heart and mind," quarreled over the distribution of money and over interpretations of obedience to the Law. . . . Debates and arguments are the signs of a church which is always being renewed by the Spirit. A perfect unanimity would be a sign of the immobility of death (1994, p. 337).

Difficulties Perceived by and About Women Religious

Women's religious life is being hampered today by "laws and inappropriate structures" requiring a movement more toward gospel radicalness and away from a deepening of the institutionalization (Starken, 1994, p. 335). In response to the over-emphasis by the church on control, many religious, both women and men, unwilling to continue to be shackled by the past, are moving more freely into the future and doing so without anxiety (Ward, 1994, p. 359).

Sr. Klara Sietmann, a Peruvian religious and president of the International Union of Superiors General, declared:

We perceive a certain lack of understanding and honest appreciation of feminine apostolic religious life, which is at times seen as an offshoot of monastic life. True to the characteristic marks of our charisms, we find the nucleus of religious consecration in our active participation in Christ's mission, continued in our world today by the church, missionary by its very nature.

We hope for new thrusts from this Synod which will encourage consecrated women to take on all their responsibilities in society and in the church. Space needs to be created which will encourage new initiatives and daring creativity in order to contribute to the building of the kingdom of God, while making full use of all the richness of religious life (Sietmann, 1994, pp. 348, 349).

The Archbishop of Quebec, speaking for the Canadian bishops, noting that women are 75 percent of the world's religious, called for the change of existing ecclesiastical structures for consecrated life for women, which would reflect the church's affirmation for equality. He said the Canadian bishops supported these specific changes, among others: to end the dichotomy often noted between the declarations of the official church regarding the dignity of women and the actual practices of discrimination; to include competent women fully within the processes of reflection and decision making, as well as in positions of real responsibility, both at the diocesan level as well as among the dicasteries of the Roman Curia; the engagement in the church of women members of institutes of consecrated life; greater involvement of religious women in the process of discernment and decision making as concerns their life as consecrated women (Couture, 1994, pp. 358-359).

Different Models of Religious Life
A number of interventions dealt with the fact that religious life has had many forms over the centuries, and that new

forms are now emerging is to be expected, and not resisted. Abbot Primate Jerome Theisen, O.S.B., noted that only since the Middle Ages were the three vows of obedience, poverty, and celibate chastity the main vows. Other forms of commitment had existed over the centuries.

> What I wish to stress today is the unity of the religious life. It is a total way of life centered on the person of Jesus. It is a complete way of life existing in the center of the church, not on its periphery. . . .It retains its ties with the searching and suffering human community. . . .Religious today are studying ways of being community in the midst of the human and church communities . . . to a total giving of self to the passionate love of Christ (1994, p. 327).

In the opening homily of the Synod, Pope John Paul II gave witness to the new forms:

> We are also witnessing the birth of new forms of consecration, particularly inside the ecclesial movements and associations, which seek to express in ways adapted to the present culture religious life's traditional tension between the contemplation of the mystery of God and the mission to our brothers and sisters (1994, p. 307).

Nature of Religious Life

While many things were said about the nature of religious life, a powerful statement about the future of feminine apostolic religious life was made by Doris Gottemoeller, R.S.M., speaking for LCWR and reflecting on the reality for women in the U.S. She identified four elements that are key to that emerging form of religious life.

In the context of the needs of today and tomorrow,

the mission of apostolic women's religious institutes should be distinguished by four characteristics: it is lay, feminine, corporate and prophetic. By *lay*, I mean that our mission is an expression of our baptismal consecration, not of clerical ordination. . . .Our radical equality as baptized Catholics is part of who we are within community, and it makes us one with the overwhelming majority of the church's membership. . . . Collaboration with other persons who share our desire to promote the reign of God's love in human hearts and social structures is a daily reality in our ministries. Second, our identification with women and as women animates and shapes our mission. *With* women, because we have made ourselves present to other women in their hopes, fears, achievements and struggles. We understand the needs of people for health care, housing, education, economic justice, political representation, moral guidance, spiritual inspiration from a women's perspective. . . .apostolic women religious make a communal commitment to mission, not in the sense of common ministry but in the sense of a common vision or priority for one's congregation. . . .the mission of apostolic women's religious life must be prophetic. . . .prophecy connotes a transparency to the divine which is the fruit of a life focused on Jesus and which is the real meaning of prophecy—speaking of God. . . .Most of all, prophecy requires a facility in drawing the gaze of the inquirer from ourselves to the Gospel which we proclaim and which animates our lives and mission (Gottemoeller, 1994, pp. 325–326).

Religious Brothers

A number of interventions were made in connection with religious brothers who are part of mixed congregations, i.e., those with both clerical and non-clerical members.

Hermann Schaluck, Minister General of the Franciscans, said that of male religious more than 34 percent are brothers. He spoke for

> the fundamental Christian equality of all religious, both male and female as well as to their co-responsibility vis-à-vis the same Gospel life. The men and women of today are particularly sensitive to this demand for familial equality and responsibility and we must discern the signs of the time in this regard. . . . we want to recover and live fully today what we already are by definition. . . .we are all brothers. . . .In this way a concept of fundamental equality will be lived out that embraces everyone in consecrated life (1994, pp. 338–340).

After the Synod

In the final message, "Consecrated Life: Expression of the Church's Spiritual Vitality," there was public affirmation of the existing reality of diversity and the value of the multiple forms of consecrated life; this life as indispensable to the church, not simply on its fringes; the deep reciprocity between mission and consecration; the importance of the charism of institutes and of their integration into a local church; the prophetic nature of religious life; the necessity for the inculturation of that life; and the uniqueness of the role of religious in the New Evangelization, including the desire for a growth in ecumenical and interreligious dialogue where religious can be of special assistance (Synod, 1994, pp. 369–374).

Fifty-five propositions were forwarded privately to the pope. While none of these were published, some examples were cited in *Origins*, based on comments and information offered by various bishops. The impression given was that the propositions were very positive, supporting openness to diversity in consecrated life on various levels. There are, apparently, calls for flexibility; for communities to have greater autonomy in regulating their internal life; for superiors of cloistered women's communities to have the same authority as male superiors. There were calls for a change in Canon Law to allow brothers to exercise leadership in communities of priests and brothers; for the promotion of the dignity of women, making better use of their gifts, allowing them to exercise more responsibility in the church, and involving them in drafting church legislation, especially when it directly affects their lives. There is a suggestion for structures for continuing dialogue between religious and the bishops.

Import of the Synod for the 21st Century

Chapters and Assemblies in religious congregations often write beautiful statements, but if there is not a commitment on the part of leaders and members to implementation, they become "beautiful words" but empty, and lead to greater alienation.

It is important that what has been said at the Synod not be words without action. There is hope for some change in that important areas of contention and dissatisfaction have been discussed at the level of a Synod. While the Synod experience appears to have been very positive, there was little from what was reported in the two major sources that deals with the needed radicalness of the future. With a few exceptions, the emphasis was more on what was and what is now, with little sense that the world we are entering may be drastically different.

We can have some hope in that the role of women has been addressed, the prophetic nature affirmed, the importance of new ministries to the poor brought forward by some of the Third World bishops.

A touching section of the final message indicated an understanding that some congregations are dying out, and that they need to be thanked for their contribution and helped in the movement toward mergers, which seems to be an acceptance that it is not the "fault" of religious or of the renewal decisions that vocations are declining, that perhaps God has some purpose in mind.

The Synod may generate new and freeing legislation, or it may become one more huge file of information in the archives somewhere. However, one can never underestimate the effect when men and women of good will come together to talk, to share, to understand more deeply. The changes that come may be obvious in the local church before they are visible in the Roman offices. The potential for new alienation if *nothing* happens is very strong. On the other hand, we, the people of God, are the ones who have to create the changes needed, and we are already doing that. Perhaps, as a result of the Synod speeches and conversations, there will be more people involved in the journey into the 21st century.

CHAPTER VII

Global Consciousness

*"Go out into the whole world
and make disciples of all nations."*

One of the major paradigm shifts now occurring is that of
increased global sense. The advances in technology and information flow, as well as the realities of increased movement among peoples and across borders, have all been
influential in this shift. What may have been one of the significant shifts of the last several centuries, the emergence of
the nation state, is being superseded by the global world,
and the concept of the new world order as it is played out
in politics, economics, culture, and religion.

Religious in the 21st century may be smaller in numbers,
but they must be much larger in vision and in concern. The
ethnic, national, and even denominational concerns will
have to be superseded by caring and interest on a global
scale. The recognition of the basic missionary nature of the
church has, over the centuries, ebbed and waned. The missionary nature was, for all intents and purposes, relegated
to certain people who would reach out to those who had
not yet heard or accepted the good news of Jesus Christ.
Since the beginning of Western colonialism in the 15th cen-

tury, a great deal of that missionary vision was delegated to the "missionary" congregations. In the latter part of the 20th century there has been a growth of interest and involvement of the laity in the overseas missions of the church, an involvement frequently made possible by the religious congregations themselves at the very time they were beginning their own analysis of the meaning of missionary today.

Since the end of Vatican II, many missionary congregations have struggled with the tension between going out and preaching the good news and the reality of the acceptance by that council of the validity of the many religions around the world. Even the social works of the missionaries—schools, health care, and development—were taken over to some extent by the foreign aid functions of many developed nations toward the developing nations. In addition, the growing self-sufficiency of the local churches in many parts of the Third World gave rise to questions about the role of foreigners in those churches. Simultaneously, the concept of mission on six continents, coming out of the meeting of the Latin American bishops, brought a subtle change in the understanding of the missionary nature of the church. At the same time the basic missionary character based in baptism was being reaffirmed, but in a broader sense.

What is emerging now is a more sophisticated new reality, more difficult to express, concerning the universality of the call of Jesus. The message is still there to be proclaimed, but we now view it in a less simplistic manner. The mission of Jesus, as he proclaimed it in Luke, is indeed for all nations, because there is injustice, poverty, illness, imprisonment, in all nations of the world. The last decade of the 20th century has witnessed a renewed surge of ethnic hatred and violence in many countries around the world. Earth, the very planet itself, is the victim of violence in terms of pollution of air, soil, and water, devastation of forests, and the extinction of species.

The consciousness that is growing is a global consciousness, a sense of the interconnectedness of the whole planet and its solar system, the species of the planet, including the human, and the theological imperative that places all within the mission mandate of Jesus. It is this global consciousness that is replacing the more limited consciousness which is hedged round with all kinds of artificial barriers of race, sex, language, and national borders. Religious life, historically, has stood over against these artificial barriers, when it functioned at its best, and has been affected by them when at its worst. We have experienced nationalism, racism, sexism in religious life at various points in our history, and some is still quite strong among religious in parts of the world. The major paradigm shift now occurring is pointing toward a one-planet understanding. While the shift is still in its early stages, indications are that it will continue and grow in strength. All areas of life—political, economic, social—are being affected as are all parts of the world.

Religious of the future will have to be very aware and very involved in these movements, fostering the developments, changing those aspects within religious life itself that are barriers. We will need to be people who "live locally but think globally." The first change needs to be in our way of thinking about the reality of the world, the church, our congregations. Many of our members are thinking differently already, but more of us need to make the shift.

One of the major areas in which the change of reality and the change of view will take place will be in the area of ministries. Whether we move from one country to another, from developed to developing nations, is far less important than the interior move from local to global thinking. Mission has always been and will continue to be a matter of vocation, not location. It is not geography that makes one missionary, but the response to the call to "love one another as I have loved you," realizing that "one another" has a global dimension. It will affect the ministries we espouse as a way of living out the mission of Jesus.

Just as in the 19th century religious reached out to help the poor, abandoned, uneducated within our own country, so the same kind of reaching out will be to all people around the globe. How we reach out will be everything from direct work with those who suffer injustice to impacting national and international policy makers to eliminate the causes of injustice and suffering. There are many avenues already open to religious in these areas. The international network of religious around the world is a solid basis for collaborative efforts of every kind. The growing international developments in the political and economic realms could provide links for religious. After almost 50 years of one major international body, the United Nations, we now see the proliferation of political and economic unions struggling to come to birth in Europe, in Africa, in the Pacific rim, in the Americas. Not all of these efforts have a focus on the poor and marginalized, but they have the potential to be influenced by aware and active citizens of all countries, among whom must be religious and church people.

Interconnectedness of All

As we think more globally, our deeper understanding of the interconnectedness of all will become more apparent. Presently, we often find ourselves pitting one cause against another: ecological concerns vs human concerns, indigenous people in rain forests vs land development, the grinding poverty of some countries as a threat to the good life in others. The important reality to be grasped is that they are all of a piece and that choosing one over the other is a hopeless strategy. Our air will not improve by eliminating the rain forests; indeed not just the lives of the indigenous people will be at risk as the forests are destroyed, but all lives will be put at risk as well. Saving whales will not mean we cannot save babies in sub-Saharan Africa. What we need is a priority sense that says we serve all best by working for all.

The world that is struggling to be born is a world based on a sense of oneness. It is a world that views unity and peace among nations as the only sensible way in an age which has learned that nuclear defense and large armies do not safeguard anyone, not even the nations who have these resources. It is a world that sees that there will be enough for everyone when sharing is a reality of the whole, not simply of some parts. It is a world that will have less and less tolerance for a distribution of goods that allows some to have great excesses of wealth while others are starving. There are still large numbers of people who do not wish to lose their comfortable life to assure that others can survive. We see every year the lists of those individuals and families who are billionaires, and in the same newspaper or television broadcast hear of thousands and hundreds of thousands dying of hunger or of preventable disease for lack of funds.

Over the history of religious life, at its holiest moments, religious have been a small prophetic body challenging the *status quo* of church or society. It has been a "voice crying in the desert" to "make straight the way of the Lord." To the extent that we are suborned by the comfortable middle-class mentality we will not be true to our calling as religious. We need to reflect deeply and honestly on the message of Jesus, the call he issued, and truly move forward on the prophetic task. The task is not necessarily or only to convert people to Jesus or to enlarge the numbers of Christians. The task is to fulfill the mission that Jesus gave us, which is captured so poignantly in Luke (4:18–19) in which Jesus spoke of his own mission:

The Spirit of God is upon me,
because God has anointed me to

preach good news to the poor.
God has sent me to proclaim release to the captives
and recovering of sight to the blind,
to set at liberty those who are oppressed,
to proclaim the acceptable year of God.

This will mean that religious congregations will be re-shaping themselves and their priorities in terms of this mission and their own specific part of it. Their ministries will reflect this shift in priorities. Educating will remain, but educating for the new world, the more Jesus world, of the future. Healing will be to heal the terrible plagues of poverty, hunger, illness, and injustice that abound in the world as well as the more traditional physical diseases. We will be doing it—if we make the shift—by our words, by our actions, and by how we live our lives, individually, communally, and congregationally.

In many ways the shifting of ministries and the sim-plification of our lifestyles, so that we too can share, will be the easier part of the task. Another area where congrega-tions will have to look for change will be in how we think about and organize and manage ourselves. One of the first things we will have to stop doing is spending so much time and energy worrying about numbers and median ages. This concern has become an obsession in the last few years in many congregations. General and Provincial Chapters spend undue amounts of time talking about voca-tions, the lack of them and how to increase them, about the aging of the group, the increased median age. This is being done at a time when people live longer, and are healthier and more active than in any previous age. In many of the founding years of congregations, life expectancy was in the area of 35 years or less, and many died young. Congregations were often the most effective when they were smaller in numbers. Partly this was due to the fact that, being small, they had to consider very carefully the best way to use their resources to effect their mission.

I often find myself at these Chapters wondering about faith and trust in God rather than in numbers. We need to get back to that idea of working as if it all depends on us, and believing as if it all depends on God. Most congregations started very small and were very small for large parts of their history. What they accomplished depended not on numbers but rather on the dedication and vision of those, however few, who were there.

Another point to consider regarding future organization is the duplication of the internal works by many congregations living and working in the same geographic areas. When we are many in numbers we find ourselves in a mentality of congregational independence. We each train our new members, organize our ministries, and care for our elderly. Only now are some of the groups beginning to question if a collaborative effort would not be more sensible. Such collaboration, especially on internal matters, could reduce the number of staff involved and eliminate some duplication of facilities for formation and for care of the elderly. There is a beginning, in terms of formation, in the intercongregational formation programs and the use of theological schools for some parts of the formative effort. However, these are mainly directed to the classrooms, and have replaced teachers. The formation staffs tend to remain much the same, and separate.

This collaborative stance needs also to impact the ministries and how we organize them. In some of the health care ministries, in past years, religious congregations found themselves not collaborating, but actually in competition with one another for "market share." There are initial efforts toward regional collaboration, but they are still much too small. In the health care field some of the collaboration is being fueled more by economic concerns and the fear of any forthcoming health care reform than from a theological aspect of mission. There is still a lingering sense that each congregation is so different from all the others that collaboration will be too difficult. Some of the current first steps toward mergers of congregations are also hopeful signs, not because they then become larger, but because they are able to eliminate unnecessary duplication and work together more effectively.

New Approaches to Governance

In individual congregations there will have to be serious consideration regarding organization, particularly how we govern ourselves. In the past, because congregations were organized according to hierarchical principles and structures (Harmer, 1993), there was a need for many levels of government and many people involved at each level. As congregations have moved to more organic models, and especially as they have recognized the intelligence and commitment of their members and their ability to make many decisions individually, by local groups or by ministry groups, some have begun simplifying the structures. Others have accepted the principles, but have continued to have top-heavy structures in relation to total numbers. A few have developed organic models but, in what is a misunderstanding of the nature of participation, have overly developed structures for members to be involved in government. Such efforts have made government larger rather than smaller. One result is that more time and energy than is truly needed is being expended on running the congregation and governing ourselves.

Some very good thinking and work are in process in terms of governance, but more has to be done. Given dedicated and intelligent members, structures can be simpler, with the number of people in leadership reduced to that needed to facilitate the movement in mission. This would require good and simple policies so each member would know where the decision could/should be made, and would be able to function within it. In order to be more accountable to one another, some congregations have increased their levels of governance and their structures, at a time when simpler approaches could work and would involve less personnel and less time. What is essential is an understanding of two things. One is that governance is for mission and should be like the skeleton in the body, very necessary, but not so large that it protrudes. The second is that the members can be empowered not only to do the work, but in many cases to make the necessary decisions involved, thus eliminating the necessity for excessive numbers of leaders, councils, and boards.

This kind of thinking is very different from what we have known, and it can raise fears. It does not mean that we do not have leaders, or that everyone does his or her own thing. When we empower members, individually and in groups, we do so to facilitate our mission more creatively, to make our ministries more effective, and to develop our members more completely. That this takes a major shift in attitude is obvious. It is difficult, and it can be scary, but it is essential if the smaller numbers in religious life are to continue to make the impact in the 21st century that we need to make. Leaders will continue to be very necessary in maintaining the unity and focus, but their roles and the work they do will differ considerably from those in the past, and even from some of the present adaptations. The answer for the future is not in adding numbers, but in empowering the religious we have.

Principles of Governance

In speaking of an organic form of governance, several principles need to be active. The first is the central concept that governance is for mission, that the purpose for government structures is to further the mission. Thus, governance is concerned with the vision, with the future and its demands, and with supporting and forwarding the ministries that have been identified as those that will most bring about the desired mission of the congregation, which is part of the mission of Jesus.

In the past, much of what was the concern of governance was in the hands of central and provincial leadership, and to a limited extent, usually the needs of individuals, in the hands of local superiors. The members were primarily responsible for carrying out the work that had been determined by higher levels. Today, and for the future, an essential principle, our second, is that there must be greater involvement by the members in the decisions related to the mission, on local or regional levels. Often those who have the most knowledge, the best understanding, are the people in the ministry or in the region. This is not to simply transfer decision making from central to regional, but to put in place an interdependent structure that recognizes the importance and the difference of central, regional, and local. The central level needs to keep in mind the whole mission, the good of the whole group. The regional and local areas focus within that on the good of the ministries in the local and regional area. These groups, then, need structures and processes that will keep them interconnected so that the whole and the parts are in healthy relationship rather than in a competitive one of struggling for power.

A third principle recognizes that there will be areas of decision making reserved to the central level because the impact will be over the whole group or large parts of it, and that other decisions will be made at regional or local levels insofar as the impact is primarily regional or local. Interdependence is the organic model's form of subsidiarity, the understanding that decisions should be made as close as possible to those affected, and involve those affected. Each group facing decision needs to consider its effect on itself, but also its effect on any other part of the whole. This builds a healthy independence, but also nurtures a sense of the whole, and a unity and interdependence, that goes well beyond structures. It moves a group far along, away from competition for resources toward a sharing of the resources, especially the scarce ones.

The number of units and the degree of complexity of structures is based on what is really needed to move the mission forward. Thus, international congregations may need more structure because of geographical dispersion, but the basic principle should hold that decisions do not go to the central level from the national unless other areas are affected. In international congregations, as in national ones, the hierarchical structures are in place due to historical developments. Both international and national groups have to do the same kind of careful analysis of their needs. It is important to have as much structure as is needed, but not more. It is possible for congregations to scale down their structures to facilitate mission without overburdening people.

Shifts in Management

Another very important aspect of a leadership whose focus is on mission is to consider if it is spending too much time on the details of management and control. As religious moved into larger and more institutional involvements, the management aspects multiplied. If religious are less involved in the future in the ownership and sponsorship of large institutional ministries (Harmer, 1994), leaders will have more time and energy for focusing on mission, the needs of mission, and the future needs for new ministries. They may be better able, then, to carry out more effectively their leadership roles, having to do with the vision, new directions, and ways to carry them out.

Much of this global thinking, reduction of emphasis on internal management, and refocus on mission will also lead religious into a greater empowerment of laity, especially in the ministries. This is already quite noticeable in the education and health fields where all levels of management and many boards of directors are heavily dependent on lay membership. New models of sponsorship are also beginning to be developed that could place much of the large institutional ministry under lay sponsorship as well as lay management. This brings us back to the role of the laity as spelled out in the Vatican II documents: being involved in the mission of the church. Thus, we are not looking at lay empowerment simply as a means to expand numbers. Beyond this concern over numbers is the growing experience in many congregations of lay people who feel a special call to serve the church more closely without embracing the evangelical life. It may well be that religious will be the main conduit for such calls to be lived out. This is not to excuse parishes and dioceses, but at this point in time religious seem more able to understand the call and more willing to try to help actualize it. As in many modes in the past, religious have another opportunity to be pioneers in this field.

National and International Influence

Another area, touched on earlier, that deserves more attention is how religious congregations can interconnect with and influence the political and economic bodies that have so much power for good or ill in the world. Already there are religious who act as representatives of certain agendas through non-governmental organizations on the United Nations; there are groups like Network who act as lobbyists with the federal government in the United States. As more of the international connections develop among nations, across continents, whether in political or economic realms, religious need to interface with these groups, bringing a vision of what is right and just. It is not enough in these cases to be in opposition to certain actions, laws, or systems. One must be able to bring alternative solutions.

One of the special efforts that international congregations could make would be to collaborate among themselves to develop a mode for interacting with the international bodies so that it is a concerted effort, non-duplicative, and consciously calling attention to the numbers of people being represented. National religious can do the same kind of interconnecting among themselves to impact the national bodies in their own countries. Over the past several decades there have been good beginnings, either by individual congregations, or by groups of religious, or through the conferences of major superiors in different countries. What religious need to become convinced of, honing the skills needed, is that a collaborative effort to influence civil governing bodies will be most effective.

Still another area that religious may wish to consider for the 21st century is the possibility, again in collaboration with one another, of consciously developing mobile groups of religious and laity capable of moving into areas of sudden emergency. We have observed over the last few decades incredible emergencies due to natural disasters, wars, and famine. Often religious have been involved in the emergency teams that move forward, but on the whole we do not have a way to respond rapidly. We often have members who are willing to go to such regions, and we spend precious time trying to organize a congregational team or trying to find another body that can provide the base.

Not every congregation or every religious has to be involved in all these ways, but as a whole group, we need to look at some of these possibilities, and others that are still to surface, to ask ourselves how can we best advance the mission of Jesus to the whole world, in a global way. How do we live the discipleship that does not exclude, that does not look away and "pass on the other side of the road" like the priest and the Levite? Often we have depended on the insights, the courage, the vision of individual members, and we must still depend on that, but we have to add to that the vision, courage, and commitment of the whole.

Ecological Globalism

Finally, it is essential that the religious of the future invest themselves in the ecological globalism of planet Earth. We do not know what the future will bring in regard to space travel, other planets, other galaxies, but the future of our own planet and solar system will depend on many of the decisions now being made. Some predicted devastations are not inevitable, though others may be irreversible. Change is possible in many areas, and sufficient change in the way we live in our world and use its wealth can bring about a healthier, safer world for all peoples. Part of thinking globally is to factor in the reality of the planet itself and its resources we share with many species. The understanding that humanity was in some way the dominator of the world, the user who did not have to consider the effects on other species or on the world itself, has been replaced with the more biblical concept of stewardship, and even with "deep ecology," which stresses that the planet is an organism in which humans are a part of nature, not apart from it.

From the indigenous peoples we are relearning our relationship to Earth. We have rediscovered that we are one of many species inhabiting this world, sharing it, responsible for it. The concept of ownership of the land was very foreign to the people who were on this continent for thousands of years before it was "discovered" by European explorers. These explorers and the people who followed brought with them the creed of dominance by humanity over land as well as over the people of the land. At present, much ecological concern is over saving the planet for the humans on it, which is a valid concern. That concern to be truly global needs to include Earth itself and *all* the species who share it. It is not a question of one species versus others, but all being for all and concerned for all. It is a very interesting exercise in mind-opening to read reflectively the many passages of the New Testament in which Jesus speaks of and interrelates with nature.

Our concern needs to be placed, also, within a theological framework that views all of nature as God's work, that sees it within a sacramental aspect. John Haught (1994) captures this often forgotten element of ecology and environmentalism when he writes of sacramentality as "an ancient theme in religion and theology" that should not be limited to the "seven sacraments."

A "sacrament," broadly understood, is anything through which we are granted a sense of the divine. And so a sacramental ecology holds that the entire cosmos sacramentally reveals God to us. Its sacramental transparency to God gives the natural world an intrinsic value that should spark in us a fervent ecological concern for its preservation. For if the biological diversity of nature is destroyed, our sense of God's grandeur will be simultaneously diminished (p. 6).

He goes on to connect this concern for the sacramentality of nature to God's fidelity to the promise for future fulfillment, to eschatology.

From biblical eschatology, then, we learn that all of reality—and that includes the natural world—is filled with promise. In all of its ambiguity nature too hints at future perfection. . . .Viewed in biblical perspective, the natural world is worth protecting because at heart it is a promise of future fulfillment. The inherent value of the cosmic present consists, at least in part, of its being an installment of the ultimate perfection announced by the good news of God's coming. Consequently, nature is not something from which to separate ourselves in order to find a final human fulfillment, but a reality to which we are everlastingly related and whose new creation we, in the spirit of St.

Paul (Romans 8:19–21), expect to occur along with the renewal of our own lives. . . .when the cosmos is viewed as promise, nature can claim our respect and conservation without requiring that we prostrate ourselves before it (pp. 6–7).

We need to enter into a covenant with the whole of our world and all its beings. Religious life, traditionally, has had a respect for asceticism. In my early years of religious life, some of those areas of asceticism had to do with fasting, with doing without some things that seemed necessary. The future will call for a new asceticism. To live simply so that others may simply live is not a choice without costs. To consider global as well as national or personal effects and to accept the consequences is a part of that new asceticism. As a child, Lent was a time to "fast" from candy or movies, and how great was the relief when Easter came! Yahweh challenges Isaiah (58:6–8) to a fasting more in keeping with what we will need in the future, if the world we are living in is to be different for us, for all the people and for the planet itself.

Is not this the fast that I choose:
to loose the bonds of injustice,
to undo the thongs of the yoke;
to let the oppressed go free,
and to break every yoke?
Is it not to share your bread with the hungry,
and bring the homeless poor into your house;
when you see the naked, to cover them,
and not to hide yourself from your own?
Then shall you call and I will answer;
you shall cry, and I will say,
Here I am.

And, we might add, the call is to do this in relation to all peoples and all species of the world. This is an asceticism worthy of the word, an asceticism whose range is limitless and whose consequences will bring God into our midst in a new way. It is an asceticism based on a positive stance toward reality rather than on a negative stance of denial. Such asceticism frees both those who exercise it and others who benefit from it. Not eating candy may be a healthier way to live for the one who is involved in denial of self; sharing bread with the hungry is the true asceticism that fosters life.

CHAPTER VIII

Creating the New

"You will be my people and I will be your God."

When the people who had left Egypt stood overlooking Canaan, the land they had been promised, they were being invited to move forward, to enter the land, to possess it. To make that step had a cost, the cost of moving in faith, not being sure what would happen or how successful they would be. What was demanded of them was a radical commitment to a future that could only be guessed at, a future that was filled with "milk and honey" but also with uncertainty. That generation chose not to move forward, not to take the risk of the unknown, not to trust in God's love and care. In so doing, they did not have the option to go back. They could not return to the flesh pots of Egypt, to the certainties they had known in their lives as slaves. That passage was closed to them. Choosing not to move forward, they were condemned to wandering in the desert for forty long years, until the unbelieving generations had died. None of them were given another chance to go into the land.

Radical Discipleship

What is needed for religious of this age to move into the next is a radical discipleship that is based in deep faith and commitment, a dual commitment to a solid spirituality linked inseparably to a social agenda that is the mission of Jesus. Already the early stages of this new age are apparent both in the growing desire and search for a spirituality both personal and communal, and a challenge to change the political, social, and economic framework of the world. The coming together of these two realities is a ". . . theological convergence . . . which will mean a centeredness on Jesus and his radical proclamation of the reign of God. . . . At the heart of Christian faith is incarnation—God becoming flesh among the poor and the outcast" (Westmoreland-White, 1994, p. 30).

What will be needed for religious, both individually and communally, is to live out the two realities as one. It is not enough to develop a deep and rich spirituality alone, nor a radical commitment to social justice alone. The two elements need to be so intertwined that one stops thinking of them as separate entities. The days of choosing between spirituality and justice, between community and mission, between prayer and ministry, need to be buried in the antiquities of our past. They were unreal divisions at best, and a deep misunderstanding of the nature of consecrated life at worst.

Westmoreland-White and the others reflecting on Dietrich Bonhoeffer and Martin Luther King, Jr., made the focus of radical discipleship, knowing

> . . . that true Christian worship and spirituality arise from the context of the world and drive the Christian into the world's suffering and pain. . . .Neither of these modern martyrs separated spirituality from social action. Their prayer lives led them deeper into the struggle for justice in the world. And their struggle

for justice drove them deeper into prayer (p. 30).

Jesus called the disciples apart for prayer and reflection at times, but when he proclaimed the mission, he made clear the connection between love of God and love of others.

Scriptural Spirituality

What is the nature of this spirituality so central to the movement into the coming age, the age of compassion? Clearly, it is going to be very Jesus-centered, in the sense that the mission of Jesus that moves us will also bring us more closely to an understanding of Jesus and his message. This is not the "rubbing noses" with Jesus that an old friend used to refer to when discussing a highly emotional, romantic concept. Rather, it is the Jesus-centeredness that sees the human and divine elements of his life and actions connected to the message he left us. Thus, it is about loving one another, loosening bonds of injustice, taking risks, being willing to go the whole way, and to pay the price of commitment.

To be Jesus-centered means that our spirituality will have to be even more scripturally based. The great interest in Scripture of the past years needs to go beyond the intellectual to the integrative realm. Scripture is not just a wonderful set of writings, stories, encouragements; it is also part of the way to deepen our understanding, our commitment, our willingness to follow Jesus. It has to move from the intellectual into the deeply integrated reality of the totality of our life in all its facets. For this to happen requires, as well, a spirit that is deeply contemplative, a spirit open to God, open to the world, ready to listen and ready to respond. It has to be a contemplative spirit that lives in the real world. To go off every so often for a retreat or period of reflection is a help to developing and maintaining the contemplative part of ourselves. For it to continue to be alive in us, this spirit has to exist in the midst of our world, in the midst of the activity to which our mission calls us, deeply involved with the people with whom and among whom we live and work. It is not the contemplation of the cloistered life, but the contemplation of the marketplace. Jesus, we are told, at one time went off across the sea of Galilee to have one of those times of quiet and reflection. When he arrived, five thousand people were already there, waiting for him. So he spoke with them, gave them the beatitudes, and then fed them! That is the contemplative spirit in the marketplace.

Our spirituality, however we develop and nurture it, has to exist and connect in an integrated way with our community, our mission, our ministries. The separation of prayer and work is artificial and completely detrimental. The spirituality of our future will need to exist in the solitary time and the communal time, in our hearts and in our works, in our words and in our actions. Parker Palmer sees action and contemplation not as separate but as parts of each other:

> I understand action to be any way that we can co-create reality with other beings and with the Spirit. . . .I understand contemplation to be any way that we can unveil the illusions that masquerade as reality and reveal the reality behind the masks (1990, p. 17).

Dying and Rebirth

How do we move forward into our Canaan? What will be some of the costs, some of the barriers that need to come down, some of the fears that have to be faced and walked through? What does radical discipleship mean for us today, as religious who are heading into the 21st century and into new forms of religious life? For one thing, we must be willing to live with uncertainty, because while we may see many of the elements we think will be part of that future, we do not know it. While we have many ideas of what the various paradigm shifts are and how they may develop, we do not have any surety about them. If there is anything we have learned over the years since the start of renewal, it is that change is inevitable. We may not know the what and how of the change, but we know that it will continue. So the first thing we need to do is to strengthen our faith and trust in God. Clinging to the past will not take us back to that past, but it may impede our movement into the future. If we resist change, we may end up simply wandering in our own desert for forty years . . . or until we die.

It is not unusual for people to fear change, to resist it. It is perhaps the most human of realities. However, this resistance has costs. Too often we count the costs of change, but fail to count the costs of resisting change. The only way to deal with the fear is to situate ourselves once again in faith in God, trust in the call of Jesus, the call we all responded to, at some point in life with a sense of total giving. If because of age, or comfort, or any other reality we have lost that sense of dependence on God, of relationship with Jesus, then we have to rediscover and reclaim it.

Along with this, we need a deep commitment to one another. To go forward on a difficult path alone is perhaps the more frightening passage. We do not have to go alone; we can go together, helping, supporting, even carrying one another at difficult moments. The picture of that motley band of Israelites moving through the desert, sometimes walking, sometimes being carried, sometimes carrying others, especially the children and the elderly, can be a symbol for religious, as we make the journey together. What we need to recapture is that pioneer spirit that we so admire as we look at our history . . . both at the congregational level and at the level of the whole of religious life. In recapturing it, we may rediscover some of the pioneering spirit that led us to religious life in our youth, that gave us not just the courage but often the delight in doing the hard and the challenging things.

We will find ourselves moving toward a more radical approach to all aspects of religious life: community, governance, ministry, spirituality. The radical aspect will put us once again in touch with both our roots at one end and our vision at the other. These two are always in a dialogic relationship when religious life is at its most vibrant. Immediately after Vatican II, in the early years of renewal, we eliminated many of the accretions that had grown up around elements of our life. Many were the less humane elements, the more restrictive regulations and procedures. However, too often we replaced them with a very humane, but basically middle-class comfort that is at odds with the depth of commitment that is required. Some of the prestige and privilege disappeared with the distinctive clothing of habits. There are still other aspects of privilege that have to go. To be with the poor, to be with the marginalized, to be in a position to exercise influence on political and economic organizations, all of these require a radical congruence between what we proclaim and how we live and act. It is far too easy for us, as humans, to rationalize the inconsistencies in our lives.

What will not work, of course, is a simplistic response. We need to develop a way of being religious that combines the authenticity of our call and way of living that call with the skill and material things required to make change happen. It is easy to give away the televisions, video machines, computers, etc., and live poorly . . . and ineffectively. It is important to know which things *truly* contribute to our ability to influence or make change, and which we like or want, but do not make a difference. It is the age-old problem of distinguishing between what we need and what we want, between what helps and what makes easy. For years, religious have debated the nature of simple living in terms of numbers and qualities of *things* and in so doing have often missed the true questions that needed to be asked.

Part of what needs to change is the sense of separation

from the people of God. So much of religious life, going back to the desert fathers and mothers, has been based on a desire to flee from "the world," from people, from the very same world and people created by God. The sense of separation at times in our history has been based on the fear of being corrupted by the world, or on the danger of being distracted from the focus on God and things spiritual. However, there have been times when the separation was subtly connected to a belief of being better, of having chosen the higher life. In the early years of the church, the widows, the virgins, the deaconesses lived within the community of the faithful, serving them both spiritually and physically (McKenna, 1967). These women were the earliest antecedents of religious life for women, predating the monastic by several centuries, and they could be the models for us today in their integration into the community and in their roles of prayer and service.

We need to be able to live in the world as it is, and live in it as deeply committed religious. This requires a clear focus on what is important, a simplicity of heart that resists the false gods, wherever they are found. To live in the midst of a people, a parish, a neighborhood, a town, to be part of the reality, aware of the wonders and the dangers, is to be religious today and for the future.

Part of what we may have to shed gradually is the dependence on large properties, investment portfolios, retirement facilities. We will still have to care for our elderly, educate our new members, support ourselves. Can we do it in a way that does not require endless rationalizations for these large estates, for retirement communities that outshine the most expensive elder care places for the laity? There is a whole generation of religious who came out of the older system, found themselves in a new mode in terms of living style, ministry, independence, and who may now need to look again at what is truly important. Will it be easy? Not at all. As I sit writing this book on a computer, knowing it is far easier, more efficient than a typewriter or a pencil and pad, I too need to ask myself, what is needed for the effectiveness of ministry and what is simply for my comfort. I may decide I need the computer but do not need the latest and the fastest and the most elegant programs and accessories to it.

Part of being with the people of God is living among them, as I have mentioned earlier, and that can create serious challenges. To live in a working-class neighborhood and live at the same level as our neighbors may be relatively simple, even if not as comfortable as we have experienced in the past. If our ministry is with suburban people, how do we live among them without being co-opted by a way of life that often is more than needed? Again, the simplistic answer is not necessarily the right one. Someone told me recently that she never bought anything she thought she needed till she had put it off for several weeks and retested the level of need. Others pursue a policy of not adding things, but only replacing. What may not work is using one's neighbors, whether in a working-class or upper-middle-class neighborhood, as the gauge of what is acceptable. We need to be a countercultural challenge to the consumerism that is based on wants rather than needs, and affects all levels of society, including the very poor.

Changes in Ministry

Our ministries have to come under the same scrutiny as our possessions. Indeed, at times ministries become possessions. We need to continually test whether the ministries we maintain are truly advancing the mission, and whether the priorities we are following are still the central ones. We can find ourselves continuing a particular ministry because we have always done it, because we built it and it is ours, because we are comfortable at it, or even because its income supports our elderly members. We need to challenge ourselves as to whether we are immersed in the wisdom of God or the wisdom of mammon. The examples may be far more subtle than they were in the past. The desert ancestors of religious life often called for a "testing of the spirit." We need to test the spirit continually, to remain sure that it is the Spirit of God, and not simply our spirit.

The challenge of the future can be both frightening and exhilarating. When many of us entered religious life initially we gave up many things: family, friends, possessions, the freedom to choose professions, marriage, and children. In our youthful enthusiasm we counted the losses as well worth what we gained in a sense of purpose, of mission, of commitment to something greater than ourselves. In our older years we may rediscover that the choices can be just as challenging, just as exciting, just as satisfying, when we take our courage in hand and move forward with good will, not being dragged into the future.

We are now past the time of renewal. That time gave us many good things and developments, but we need to move beyond it. Refounding is often spoken of, but few of us can see how it may occur, beyond suggestions of a small group starting something new or a new segment within the old. This may happen. In the past, new forms of religious life emerged and grew while the older models remained. Both old and new co-existed, sometimes for centuries. If there is a refounding, it cannot simply be a slight variation. The shift from the monastic to the mendicant was a major change. The later shift to the apostolic religious was a major break. However, in both of these changes, some of the earlier monastic elements were retained, even when it was questionable whether the retention strengthened the new. If we refound, we must do it not by adaptation, not by incremental change, but by a radical shift that matches the radicality of the gospel and of the social changes that are occurring.

Transformation: Key to the Future

The only thing that will really move us into the future is transformation. This calls for a deep and essential conversion of life and of our whole reality. It was what was being asked of the Israelites; it is what is being asked of religious. Conversion, transformation, means to take the risk, to choose to live differently, and then to live authentically with that new reality.

C.G. Jung, the psychiatrist, often spoke and wrote of the second half of life as being a time for a new movement, a movement toward individuation, of becoming the person one was meant to be and of being in union with the Self, which for Jung meant the Divine. Religious life may be entering that second half of life, the time of transformation, of moving toward the integration and unity with the divine in a new way. For Jung, that stage meant the person moving toward the integration of wisdom as well. Religious life in the 21st century may be on the threshold of that second half of life, the movement to transformation and to wisdom.

What is needed for our journey? Exactly the same thing that Moses needed to make the journey: the recognition of God's continuing presence. At one point in the journey out of Egypt, when God threatened to withdraw, Moses said he would not go on, that he could not do it without God's presence. Juliana Casey speaks of it in these terms:

> What kept Moses going was the constant presence of God. Only if God shared the people's experience could they go on. . . .The God of Exodus is revealed to us as one deeply immersed in human life, powerfully engaged in a people's suffering, determined to know and be known by human beings. This is a God who goes with the people, who calls, cajoles, and commands a people to freedom, to recognition, and to worship (1991, pp. 5-6).

What this is, in reality, is a deep and true sense of community, of the *ekklesia*, being together with God and with one another, as people who are being called and led and who will help one another on the way, a sense of being part of a very important journey. Once we have eliminated the separateness that still exists to some extent among religious, we may find that the people who are on the way to this promised land, to this transformed reality, are many more than we might expect, and we may find them in many familiar and unfamiliar places. To believe one is alone is one of the most devastating experiences for human beings. We are not alone; there is a great mob of people on the journey into Canaan.

What we may rediscover, as many have already, is an excitement that makes one "get out of bed in the morning" (MacKinnon, 1993), a rediscovery of the early enthusiasm of the founders, of our own enthusiasm in our youth when we believed and knew that anything was possible, the enthusiasm of many generations of religious who heard the call in their age and responded, against all earthly wisdom, all sense and sensibility, who simply knew that God would be with them. Jesus spoke of putting one's hand to the plow and not looking back. It is time for religious to put their hands to the plow and to look ahead with courage and determination and with hearts afire for the work of the Lord, the work of the mission of Jesus. We need to remember the promise: "I will be with you all days unto the end of the world." A deep conversion, a belief in the continuing presence of God—these will be the aids we will have that will make the journey into Canaan possible. It will be what makes our future one that is truly in the hands of the Lord. It will root us in the Lord and the reality of the promised land, and give us the courage to go toward that unknown land with its "milk and honey," but also with its "giants." It will help us to live courageously with the unknown and to exult in the challenges, the dangers, and the grace-filled experiences of God with us.

Entry into Canaan

"O you of little faith, why did you doubt?"

[Moses said to the people:] For you are a people holy to the Lord your God; the Lord your God has chosen you out of all the peoples on earth to be his people, his treasured possession.

It was not because you were more numerous than any other people that the Lord set his heart on you and chose you—for you were the fewest of all peoples. It was because the Lord loved you and kept the oath that he swore to your ancestors, that the Lord has brought you out with a mighty hand, and redeemed you from the house of slavery, from the hand of Pharaoh king of Egypt. Know therefore that the Lord your God is God, the faithful God who maintains covenant loyalty with those who love him and keep his commandments, to a thousand generations, and who repays in their own person those who reject him. He does not delay but repays in their own person those who reject him. Therefore, observe diligently the commandment—the statutes, and the ordinances—that I am commanding you today (Deuteronomy 7:6–11).

For the Lord will again take delight in prospering you,

just as he delighted in prospering your ancestors, when you obey the Lord your God by observing his commandments and decrees that are written in this book of the law, because you turn to the Lord your God with all your heart and with all your soul.

Surely, this commandment that I am commanding you today is not too hard for you, nor is it too far away. It is not in heaven, that you should say, "Who will go up to heaven for us, and get it for us so that we may hear it and observe it?" Neither is it beyond the sea, that you should say, "Who will cross to the other side of the sea for us, and get it for us so that we may hear it and observe it?" No, the word is very near to you; it is in your mouth and in your heart for you to observe (Deuteronomy 30:9–14).

When Moses had finished speaking all these words to all Israel, he said to them: "I am now one hundred twenty years old. I am no longer able to get about, and the Lord has told me, 'You shall not cross over this Jordan.' The Lord your God himself will cross over before you. He will destroy these nations before you, and you shall dispossess them. Joshua also will cross over before you, as the Lord promised. The Lord will do to them as he did to Sihon and Og, the kings of the Amorites, and to their land, when he destroyed them. The Lord will give them over to you and you shall deal with them in full accord with the command that I have given to you. Be strong and bold; have no fear or dread of them, because it is the Lord your God who goes with you; he will not fail you or forsake you."

Then Moses summoned Joshua and said to him in the sight of all Israel: "Be strong and bold, for you are the one who will go with this people into the land that the Lord has sworn to their ancestors to give them; and you will put them in possession of it. It is the Lord who goes before you. He will be with you; he will not fail you or forsake you. Do not fear or be dismayed" (Deuteronomy 31:1–8).

Then Moses went up from the plains of Moab to Mount Nebo, to the top of Pisgah, which is opposite Jericho, and the Lord showed him the whole land: Gilead as far as Dan, all Naphtali, the land of Ephraim and Manasseh, all the land of Judah as far as the Western Sea, the Negeb, and the Plain—that is, the valley of Jericho, the city of palm trees—as far as Zoar. The Lord said to him, "This is the land of which I swore to Abraham, to Isaac, and to Jacob, saying, 'I will give it to your descendants'; I have let you see it with your eyes, but you shall not cross over there." Then Moses, the servant of the Lord, died there in the land of Moab, at the Lord's command. He was buried in a valley in the land of Moab, opposite Beth-peor, but no one knows his burial place to this day. Moses was one hundred twenty years old when he died; his sight was unimpaired and his vigor had not abated. The Israelites wept for Moses in the plains of Moab thirty days; then the period of mourning for Moses was ended.

Joshua son of Nun was full of the spirit of wisdom, because Moses had laid his hands on him; and the Israelites obeyed him, doing as the Lord had commanded Moses.

Never since has there arisen a prophet in Israel like Moses, whom the Lord knew face to face. He was unequaled for all the signs and wonders that the Lord sent him to perform in the land of Egypt, against Pharaoh and all his servants and his entire land, and for all the mighty deeds and all the terrifying displays of power that Moses performed in the sight of all Israel (Deuteronomy 34:1–12).

Immediately he made the disciples get into the boat and go on ahead to the other side, while he dismissed the crowds. And after he had dismissed the crowds, he went up the mountain by himself to pray. When evening came, he was there alone, but by this time the boat, battered by the waves, was far from the land, for the wind was against them. And early in the morning he came walking toward them on the sea. But when the disciples saw him walking on the sea, they were terrified, saying, "It is a ghost!" And they cried out in fear. But immediately Jesus spoke to them and said, "Take heart, it is I; do not be afraid."

Peter answered him, "Lord, if it is you, command me to come to you on the water." He said, "Come." So Peter got out of the boat, started walking on the water, and came toward Jesus. But when he noticed the strong wind, he became frightened, and beginning to sink, he cried out, "Lord, save me!" Jesus immediately reached out his hand and caught him, saying to him, "You of little faith, why did you doubt?" When they got into the boat, the wind ceased. And those in the boat worshiped him, saying, "Truly you are the Son of God."

When they had crossed over, they came to land at Gennesaret. After the people of that place recognized him, they sent word throughout the region and brought all who were sick to him, and begged him that they might touch even the fringe of his cloak; and all who touched it were healed (Matthew 14:22–36).

Bibliography

(These publications include not only those that I have quoted from in this volume, but those that have influenced me.)

Abbott, Walter M., S.J. (ed.).*The Documents of Vatican II*. New York: America Press, 1966.

Arbuckle, Gerald A. *Out of Chaos: Refounding Religious Congregations*. Mahwah, N.J.: Paulist Press, 1988.

Arbuckle, Gerald A. "Prophecy or Restorationism in Religious Life." In: *Review for Religious*, v. 52, 1993, pp. 326–339.

Azevedo, Marcello G. "Mission and Religious Life." In: *UISG Bulletin*, no. 83, 1990, pp. 36–48.

Beaudry, Susan, and Edwin L. Keel. "Journeying to God Together." In: *Review for Religious*, v. 53, 1994, pp. 440–441.

Berry, Thomas. "Apostolic Women Religious as a Voice of the Earth." In: *UISG Bulletin*, no. 93, 1993, pp. 45–55.

Bifet, Juan Esquerda. "Church Renewal for a New Evangelization." In: *UISG Bulletin*, no. 83, 1990, pp. 3–22.

Boff, Leonardo. *Church: Charism and Power; Liberation Theology and the Institutional Church*. London: SCM Press, 1985.

Boff, Leonardo. *Ecclesiogenesis: The Base Communities Reinvent the Church*. Maryknoll, N.Y.: Orbis Books, 1986.

Brueggemann, Walter. *The Prophetic Imagination*. Philadelphia: Fortress Press, 1983.

Cada, Lawrence, et al. *Shaping the Coming Age of Religious Life*. Worcester, Mass.: Seabury Press, 1985.

Capra, Fritjof. *The Tao of Physics: an Exploration of the Parallels Between Modern Physics and Eastern Mysticism*. New York: Bantam Books, 1975.

Capra, Fritjof, David Steindl-Rast, and Thomas Matus. *Belonging to the Universe: Explorations on the Frontiers of Science and Spirituality*. San Francisco: HarperSanFrancisco, 1991.

Casey, Juliana. *Food for the Journey: Theological Foundations of the Catholic Healthcare Ministry*. St. Louis: Catholic Health Association, 1991.

Chandler, Russell. *Racing Toward 2001: The Forces Shaping America's Religious Future.* Grand Rapids: Zondervan, 1992.

Chittister, Joan. *Women, Ministry and the Church.* Mahwah, N.J.: Paulist Press, 1983.

Chittister, Joan. "Religious Life is Still Alive, but Far From the Promised Land." In: *National Catholic Reporter,* February 18, 1994, pp. 13–17.

Chopra, Deepak, M. D. *Ageless Body, Timeless Mind: The Quantum Alternative to Growing Old.* New York: Harmony Books, 1993.

Cleveland, Harlan. "Ten Keys to World Peace." In: *The Futurist,* v. 28, 1994, pp. 15–17.

Couture, Maurice. "Consecrated Women: Equality in the Church." In: *Origins,* v. 24, no. 21, 1994, pp. 358–359.

DeThomasis, Louis. *Imagination: A Future for Religious Life.* Winona, Minn.: The Metanoia Group, 1992.

Dossey, Larry. *Healing Words.* San Francisco: HarperSanFrancisco, 1993.

Dowling, Kevin. Intervention. In: *Origins,* v.24, no. 18, 1994, p. 308.

Etzioni, Amitai. *The Spirit of Community: Rights, Responsibilities, and the Communitarian Agenda.* New York: Crown, 1993.

Fiand, Barbara. *Living the Vision: Religious Vows in an Age of Change.* New York: Crossroad, 1990.

Foley, Nadine (ed.). *Claiming Our Truth: Reflections on Identity by United States Women Religious.* Washington, D.C.: LCWR, 1988.

Fuellenbach, John. "Religious life in the year 2000." In: *UISG Bulletin,* no. 83, 1990, pp. 49–60.

Galilea, Segundo. *The Beatitudes: to Evangelize as Jesus Did.* Maryknoll, N.Y. : Orbis Books, 1984.

Gelatt, H. B. "Future Sense: Creating the Future." In: *The Futurist,* v. 27, no. 5, pp. 9–13.

Gottemoeller, Doris. "Apostolic Women Religious: Identity and Mission." In: *Origins,* v. 24, no. 19, 1994, pp. 325–326.

Gottemoeller, Doris. "Synod Update: Doris Gottemoeller, RSM, reflects." In: *LCWR Update,* October 1994, no pagination.

Greenleaf, Robert K. *Servant Leadership: A Journey into the Nature of Legitimate Power and Greatness.* New York: Paulist Press, 1977.

Harmer, Catherine M. "Internationality: Intentional or Accidental." In: *Review for Religious,* v. 52, 1993, pp. 111–118.

Harmer, Catherine M. "Multi–culturalism in Religious Life Today." In: *Review for Religious,* v. 52, 1993, pp. 764–772.

Harmer, Catherine M. "Religious, the Laity, and the Future of Catholic Institutions." In: *Review for Religious,* v. 53, 1994, pp. 375–385.

Haught, John F. "Three Views of Ecological Theology." In: *Pax*

Christi USA, v. XIX, 1994, pp. 5–7.

Hennessy, Anne. "Galilean Perspectives on Religious Life." In: *Review for Religious,* v. 52, 1993, pp. 247–258.

Hogan, William F. "Missionary by Nature." In: *Review for Religious,* v. 53, 1994, pp. 397–401.

Holland, Joe, and Peter Henriot. *Social Analysis: Linking Faith and Justice.* Washington, D.C.: Center for Concern, 1980.

Hostie, Raymond, S.J. *Vie et Mort des Ordres Religieux.* Paris: Desclée de Brouwer, 1972.

Jeanrond, Werner G. "Leadership and Authority." In: *The Way,* v. 32, 1992, pp. 187–195.

John Paul II. "Homily for the Opening of the Synod." In: *Origins,* v. 24, no. 18, 1994, pp. 305–307.

Johnson, Elizabeth A. "Between the Times: Religious Life and the Postmodern Experience of God." In: *Review for Religious,* v. 53, 1994, pp. 6–28.

Johnson, Elizabeth A. "Discipleship: Root Model of the Life Called 'Religious.'" In: *Review for Religious,* v. 42, 1983, pp. 864–872.

Keenan, Marjorie. "Peace with God—Peace with all Creation." In: *UISG Bulletin,* no. 83, 1990, pp. 23–35.

Kidder, Rushworth M. *Reinventing the Future: Global Goals for the 21st Century.* Cambridge, Mass.: MIT Press, 1989.

Kidder, Rushworth M. "Universal Human Values: Finding an Ethical Common Ground." In: *The Futurist,* no. 4, 1994, pp. 8–14.

Kuhn, Thomas S. *The Structure of Scientific Revolutions.* Chicago: University of Chicago Press, 1962.

Land, George, and Beth Jarman. *Break-point and Beyond: Mastering the Future—Today.* New York: HarperCollins, 1993.

Land, George. "Breakpoint Change Necessitates Partnerships." In: *Health Progress,* v. 75, no. 6, 1994, p. 34.

Leddy, Mary Jo. *Reweaving Religious Life: Beyond the Liberal Model.* Mystic, Conn.: Twenty-Third Publications, 1990.

Letourneau, Marguerite. "Feminine Apostolic Religious Life: New Vitality and New Challenges." In: *UISG Bulletin,* no. 92, 1993, pp. 7–16.

Letourneau, Marguerite. "The Consecrated Life and its Role in the Church and in the World: An Overview of Responses to the Lineamenta." In: *UISG BULLETIN,* no. 94, 1994, pp. 9–18.

Lozano, John M. *Discipleship: Toward an Understanding of Religious Life.* Chicago: Claret Center for Resources in Spirituality, 1980.

McCann, Patricia. "An Identity Dilemma: Standing with the Poor." In: *Review for Religious,* v. 52, 1993, pp. 428–431.

McKenna, M. *Women of the Church: Role and Renewal.* New York: Kenedy, 1967.

McManus, William E. "The Right of Catholics to Govern the

Church." In: *America*, v. 167, no. 15, 1992, pp. 374–378.
MacKinnon, Mary Heather. "Why Should Religious get up in the Morning?" In: *National Catholic Reporter*, v. 29, no. 16, 1993, pp. 13–14.
Markham, Donna. "Communities of Hope." In: *Review for Religious*, v. 51, 1992, pp. 815–822.
Masini, Eleonora B. "A World in Transformation: A Challenge for Women Religious." In: *UISG Bulletin*, no. 93, 1993, pp. 3–23.
Milligan, Mary. "Theological Reflection on our Thirty-year Post-conciliar Experience of Feminine Apostolic Religious Life." In: *UISG Bulletin*, no. 94, 1994, pp. 19–25.
Moreno, Juan Ramon. "Church of the Poor." In: *Review for Religious*, v. 51, 1992, pp. 486–495.
Moreno, Juan Ramon. "Religious Life in the Puebla Document." In: *Review for Religious*, v. 51, 1992, pp. 707–715.

Neal, Marie Augusta. *Catholic Sisters in Transition: From the 1960s to the 1980s*. Wilmington, Del.: Michael Glazier, 1984.
Nygren, David J., et al. "Religious-leadership Competencies." In: *Review for Religious*, v. 52, 1993, pp. 390–417.
Nygren, David J., and Miriam D. Ukeritis. "The Religious Life Futures Project: Executive Summary." In: *Review for Religious*, v. 52, 1993, pp. 6–55.

O'Brien, Anne. "The Role of Active Apostolic Women Religious." In: *Review for Religious*, v. 49, 1990, pp. 213–219.

Padberg, John W. "In the Midst of the Times: Religious Life and the Ever–present Experience of the World." In: *Review for Religious*, v. 53, 1994, pp. 166–181.
Palmer, Parker J. *The Active Life: A Spirituality of Work, Creativity, and Caring*. San Francisco: Harper & Row, 1990.
Pohl, Frederick. "The Uses of the Future." In: *The Futurist*, v. 27, 1993, pp. 9–12.
Popko, Kathleen. "Contemplating Religious Life's Future." In: *Origins*, v. 21, no. 12, 1991, pp. 219–224.
Puerto, Mercedes Navarro. "Women Living Apostolic Religious Life: A Narration of Paradoxes." In: *UISG Bulletin*, no. 95, 1994, pp. 33–44.

Quigley, Carol (ed.). *Turning Points in Religious Life*. Westminster, Md.: Christian Classics, 1988.

Radcliffe, Timothy. "Dialogue and Communion." In: *Religious Life Review*, v. 33, no. 169, 1994, pp. 336–338.
Regan, Thomas J. "New Needs. . . New Paradigms: The Changing Character of Religious Life." In: *Review for Religious*, v. 49, 1990, pp. 220–226.
Reutemann, Charles. "Religious Life Spirituality in the Year 2010."

In: *Review for Religious*, v. 49, 1990, pp. 185–198.

Ruffing, Janet K. "Leadership a New Way: If Christ is Growing in Us." In: *Review for Religious*, v. 53, 1994, pp. 486–497.
Ruffing, Janet K. "Leadership a New Way: Women, Power, and Authority." In: *Review for Religious*, v. 53, 1994, pp. 326–339.
Ruffing, Janet K. "Seeing in the Dark." In: *Review for Religious*, v. 51, 1992, pp. 236–248.

Schillebeeckx, Edward. *Ministry: Leadership in the Community of Jesus Christ*. New York: Crossroad, 1984.
Schneiders, Sandra M. *New Wineskins: Re-imagining Religious Life Today*. New York: Paulist Press, 1986.
Schumacher, E.F. *A Guide for the Perplexed*. New York: Harper & Row, 1977.
Schweickert, Jeanne. *Toward the New Millenium: A National Vision of Religious Life*. Chicago: Convergence, 1992.
Sietmann, Klara. "Assuring Consecrated Women's Roles in the Church." In: *Origins*, v. 24, no. 20, 1994, pp. 348–349.
Sine, Tom. *Wild Hope*. Dallas: Word Publishing, 1991.
Sobrino, Jon. *The True Church and the Poor*. Maryknoll, N.Y.: Orbis Books, 1984.
Starken, Elizabeth. "Mission and Radical Commitment." In: *Religious Life Review*, v. 33, no. 169, 1994, pp. 334–336.
Stevens, Maryanne. "The Shifting Order of Religious Life in our Church." In: *Review for Religious*, v. 48, 1989, pp. 515–529.
Synod. "Consecrated Life: Expression of Church's Spiritual Vitality." In: *Origins*, v. 24, no. 22, 1994, pp. 369–374.

Theisen, Jerome. "The Vows in Context: A Total Way of Life." In: *Origins*, v. 24, no. 19, 1994, pp. 326–327.
Theobald, Robert. *The Rapids of Change: Social Entrepreneurship in Turbulent Times*. Indianapolis: Knowledge Systems, 1987.
Theobald, Robert. *Turning the Century: Personal and Organizational Strategies for Your Changed World*. Indianapolis: Knowledge Systems, 1992.
Turner, Mary Daniel. "Power: Its Ethic and Ethos." In: *Network Connection*, v. 22, no. 2, 1994, pp. 10–11.
Turner, Mary Daniel. "TheFuture of Religious Life." In: *Ink-Links*, Apr. 28, May 5, May 12, 1993, pp. 1–15.

Ward, Aloysius. "The Future of Consecrated Life." In: *Religious Life Review*, v. 33, no. 169, 1994, pp. 359–361.
Westmoreland-White, M., et al. "Disciples of Incarnation." In: *Sojourners*, v. 23, 1994, pp. 26–30.
Wittberg, Patricia. *Creating a Future for Religious Life: A Sociological Perspective*. Mahwah, N.J.: Paulist Press, 1991.

Of Related Interest...

Reweaving Religious Life
Beyond the Liberal Model
Mary Jo Leddy
Challenges religious to reimage their lives and ministries, looking at
Gospel values rather than social/cultural emphases.

ISBN: 0-89622-440-6, 200 pp

Christianity & Feminism in Conversation
Regina A. Coll
Coll calls on readers to revise and reclaim the symbols, myths and
metaphors of Christianity from a feminist perspective.

ISBN: 0-89622-579-8, 224 pp

The Hope for Wholeness
A Spirituality for Feminists
Katherine Zappone
Zappone examines the origins and future directions of feminist
spirituality.

ISBN: 0-89622-495-3, 208 pp

WomanGifts
Biblical Models for Forming Church
Sister Pamela Smith, SS.C.M., Art by Sister Virginia DeWan, SS.C.M.
Each of the spiritual portraits in the book is introduced by a Scripture
citation and includes a prayer and questions for reflection or
discussion.

ISBN: 0-89622-572-0, 144 pp

Available at religious bookstores or from:
TWENTY-THIRD PUBLICATIONS
P.O. Box 180 • Mystic, CT 06355
1-800-321-0411
Fax: 1-800-572-0788

In Ireland:
The Columba Press
93 The Rise, Mount Merrion
Blackrock, Co Dublin
Phone: Dublin 283-2954
Fax: Dublin 288-3770